MW00489790

117 Things
I Did in the Year After My
Son Died: Stories About
Dealing With Grief
By Brent Hickenbottom

For my family...and my friends that have become family.

Thanks for letting me tell these stories...

117 Things
I Did in the Year After My Son Died: Stories About Dealing With Grief
By Brent Hickenbottom

Grayden Steele Hickenbottom was born June 24, 2010 in Quincy, IL. My wife Jamie and I had been praying for him for a little over a year before we found out he was coming.

I will never forget the feeling I experienced when the doctor said, "It's a boy." We chose to be surprised…and it was a great day. Our family was growing, and we were thrilled.

Grayden was happy and healthy, for the most part. He had his fair share of ear infections and experienced febrile (or fever induced) seizures. But, we did our due diligence and were repeatedly told that he did not have a seizure disorder and were assured that although his seizures "would be scary to watch," they were not dangerous.

On Monday, January 28, when he was just a bit over two and a half years old, Grayden went down for his nap a happy and healthy boy, and never woke up.

After six months, in which the medical examiner's office kept sending more slides out to try to find a cause of death, we received the autopsy results that revealed a cause of death due to "complications from a seizure disorder."

Confused by this, I contacted my brother-in-law, who is a forensic pathologist, to ask if this indicated that something was identified that would reveal a seizure disorder through the autopsy process. His response was simple, "No." He said that because we had reported a history of seizure that it was ruled accordingly. He went on to say that had we not indicated a history of seizure, it would have most likely been ruled "undetermined."

My gut tells me he had a seizure and his little body was just in the wrong position and the wrong time—a fluke. We are dealing with the fact that our boy is gone and we don't understand why.

Nonetheless, this particular day changed our lives forever.

In the time since, we have experienced some painful "firsts," a few bittersweet challenges and plenty of stories that helped us to realize we were going to be "okay."

We prepped ourselves for a rough first year—and we made it through. I wanted to highlight a few of the ups and downs from that year in hopes it might shed some light on our journey. Not because we handled it flawlessly, but instead because we didn't.

Several people have asked us what to say (and what not to say) if they encounter a similar situation in the future. In hearing these questions, we recognized this is an impossible situation for everyone involved. It is hard to see your family and friends hurting…and fear creeps in to your decision-making. The fear of saying or doing the wrong thing often trumps the desire to be helpful. What makes things worse is helplessness seems to trump every other potential feeling and emotion.

We struggled—and it is important for people to realize we struggled. Not because we want the sympathy (the last thing we want is pity) but instead, because struggle is inevitable in this situation and recognizing this leads to better a understanding of the process.

We did some things that were beneficial to our potential healing. We also did things that were quite detrimental to that same goal. We are hardly a model for how to combat and defeat grief—this is illustrated by the fact that we still experience sadness and grief on a daily basis.

In an attempt to help others have a truer sense of the grief of losing a young child, I wanted to put some things down on paper. I hope you can find some peace and understanding as you read about our family in the year following Grayden's death.

Planned a
themed funeral

When our pastor came to our house to talk about the specifics for Grayden's funeral, we had a pretty good idea what we wanted it to look like. I don't remember ever sitting down and talking about it with my wife, Jamie, in a formal manner, but somehow we just knew-- and it came together beautifully.

Our requests were simple...and this is what we told people:

> *"Please come help us celebrate the life of our sweet, little boy. Visitation will be at Collier's Funeral Home at 3400 N. Lindbergh from 4:00-8:00 p.m., Wednesday evening Funeral services will be at The Journey-Hanley Road Thursday at 11:00a.m.*
>
> *Please DO NOT WEAR BLACK...we want to celebrate our little guy and provide him with a day worthy of his attention. Please come in a character shirt or wear something fun-- Teenage Mutant Ninja Turtles, Superman, Dora The Explorer... whatever speaks "two year old" to you.*
>
> *We want to pump both places with color and positive energy.*
>
> *We will be casual and in clothes he would approve of and ask you to do the same!*
>
> *This will be a day of celebration for the time we had with him and we will praise God that he is now by his side."*

We had people in footy pajamas, bright colors and character shirts. It was brilliant. We wanted people to match us, to match him. After all, he would be buried in a Teenage Mutant "Engine" Turtles shirt.

I remember saying, "We want this to be something that if it were not a funeral, and if he were here, that he would enjoy." I was worried for a short period of time that this was not an appropriate way to have a celebration of life ceremony, but that feeling lasted about three minutes.

Instead of flowers, we placed large bouquets of bright balloons at the front of the church along with large photo collages and some of his toys. One of our friends is a professional entertainer known as "Juggling Jeff." We were so grateful he re-arranged his schedule to be able to perform for kids at Grayden's service. It was such an amazing bonus.

In talking specifics with our pastor, we had a clear idea of what we wanted the ceremony to look like. Lots of music, biblically centered and driven message and positive energy. We started talking…and were able to be specific with what we wanted. I remember being nervous about our plan—fearing it would not be Christ centered enough. However, as we pitched our ideas to him (with the asterisk in place that we wanted him to trump us if our ideas were not appropriate) his response was simple, "It's perfect…it is exactly what we (will) do."

His message was brilliant…it was exactly what we needed to hear. Our pastor, Jeremy Irwin, gave everyone in attendance a message that they will not soon forget. His words were perfect and his metaphors powerful. Please enjoy his words:

"Thank you to everyone for being here as we both celebrate the beautiful life and grieve the tragic death of Grayden Hickenbottom. We have already heard a wonderful recounting of his 2.5 years from his proud and loving parents. Our hearts go out to them today. And in the days to come they will need us to surround them with prayers and our presence. This is an unthinkable loss. A parent's worst nightmare. It's hard to find words to say, so we turn to God's words.

The God of the Bible tells us that we should grieve Grayden with hope because of Jesus. That somehow those two seemingly opposite feelings can coexist in our hearts. Grief and hope. So today I want to talk about Grayden, grief and the hope of Jesus.

First, grief. God would not have us pretend that this doesn't hurt. It is awful. It is terrible. On Monday morning, Grayden seemed like a perfectly healthy little boy. Monday afternoon, he died in his sleep.

Death is an evil intruder in God's world. It is an enemy. And our lives have once again been stung by death. When Jesus' friend Lazarus died, the Bible says Jesus wept and was angry. That is how God feels about death. And it is right and good for us to feel the same way.

Brent, in talking with you, you said many times that you were mentally scrolling through all of the "what ifs" and "if onlys". And they weren't in reference to "Could I have done something to save him?" because we know that you couldn't have. Rather, you were grieving both all of the lost joys of Grayden's 2.5 years and all of the lost possibilities of watching him grow up. Brent and Jamie, you were both so excited to have him play with Jayce, teach him about music, play catch, take him to school, see him graduate, see him get married. So we grieve the loss of these things. We grieve the loss of a life cut short. And we don't know why. And it hurts and there is no need to pretend otherwise. Some wounds in this life will never fully heal. Some holes will never get filled. Some of you really need to hear when God says, it's okay to hurt – to weep with those who weep in this broken, broken world where rambunctious little boys lay unmoving in caskets. But you also need to hear when God says there is real hope because of Jesus. We grieve with hope.

So what hope does God have for us today?

Hope for Grayden, Hope for the Hickenbottoms, Hope for Any and All who trust Jesus.

Hope for Grayden: I want to quote Jesus from Mark 10:13-14

"And the crowds were bringing children to him that he might bless them, and the disciples rebuked the crowds. But when Jesus saw it, he was indignant, and said to them, 'Let the children come to me; do not hinder them, for to such belongs the kingdom of God'."

Notice Jesus' love for His children. We might get the impression that these are 8-10 year olds who are running to Jesus but in Luke's account he makes it clear that these are infants, young children, some of whom are unable to run to Jesus, unable to speak the name of Jesus, unable to walk an aisle, sign a card or articulate a prayer—they had to be carried to the arms of Jesus. They could not embrace Jesus but Jesus moved to embrace them. This is how it is with young children. They may not be able to demonstrate faith in Christ or run to Jesus but Jesus shows us here that He runs to them, that He embraces them. Our hope from Jesus for Grayden is that though he was young and barely able to articulate belief in God… that God loved and embraced him. I love Grayden's prayer that the Hickenbottoms shared.

"Jesus, I'm sorry I hit Jayce. Amen."

Precious to God are the prayers of a 2.5 year old. And it reminds us that the Gospel has never been about keeping morals but about asking for mercy, the mercy of Jesus.

Jesus promises the Kingdom to children. Not because they deserve it, but because He is full of mercy. So what happened on Monday is that Grayden went to sleep having known the embrace of his parents, he died, and he woke up in the embrace of Jesus. The Kingdom of Heaven belongs to such as these. That is the source of our hope- the promise of Jesus.

Grayden is right now with God. Consequently, he is happier than the happiest person on earth. The fact that Grayden missed earth's pleasures of marriage and children and friends does not cause him the slightest regret. He took a shorter route to the One, about whom the Bible says, in God's presence there is fullness of joy, at His right hand are pleasures evermore. He's in paradise with God.

See, it is right to grieve because we will not see Grayden grow up here. But we have hope, because Jesus has appointed that Grayden will grow up with Him, in the Kingdom of God.

That's our hope for Grayden, what is our hope for the Hickenbottoms?

Not long ago I read another pastor's account of his visit to the home of a congregant and on their floor was a stone engraved with the words, "the moon is round." This was of course peculiar so he asked what it meant. The woman explained that she had a young friend who had died of cancer when she was only 14 and that during her 2 year struggle, she kept a journal of Bible verses that comforted her in her suffering. After the girl died, friends and family began to read her journal and in the middle of the journal there was an index card with no verse, just the statement "the moon is round." Of course they were initially as confused as the pastor but eventually the meaning became clear: When it is dark and only a sliver of the moon is showing, what do you know? You know that, though you cannot see it, the moon is round. This teenage girl believed that though she could only see a sliver of God's loving purposes and intentions in everything that was happening to her, she knew that God was gracious and good.

Brent and Jamie, we do not know the entirety of God's purposes. We don't know why this and other things have happened to you. But we know and you know the moon is round. God loves you. He is good and gracious. Romans 5 tells us that "God demonstrated His love for us in this, while were still sinners, Christ died for us." God has proven His love. He did not spare His own Son, but gave Him up for us.

But in this life we have countless troubles and we often see only a sliver of his loving purpose, right?

God tells us to walk by faith, not by sight.

The moon is round.

Now we see in a mirror dimly… but a day is surely coming when we shall see reality truly, when we shall see Jesus Himself face-to-face. A day is coming when your temporary separation from Grayden will be no more. You will be reunited with him in a renewed world – a world in which God Himself has promised that there will be no more sin, sickness, sorrow, suffering or death… because God Himself will banish them all forever. God will dwell in our midst once again.

That is how you can grieve with hope.

The apostle Paul, who also suffered greatly, said it like this, "For I consider that our present sufferings are not even worth comparing to the glory that will be revealed."

My prayer is that God would comfort you heart with these truths such that in future years when people ask you about your family, you can say, with confidence.

We have two boys. Grayden and Jayce. Grayden is with Jesus in heaven. And one day we will join Him there because we trust Jesus and Jesus has promised it would be so.

What about the rest of us? What is our hope?

Well, the good news of Christianity is that Jesus Himself faced two of our greatest enemies for us – sin and death. On the cross, Jesus took upon Himself the penalty that our evil thoughts, words and deeds deserve. He was punished by God in our place, even though He was innocent. Not only that, Jesus entered into death in order to defeat it Himself. Jesus took our sin and he took death and he absorbed them into Himself. He swallowed them whole down to the very last drop. So that… for any who come to Him with faith, who ask Him to save us from our sins and death… Jesus grants us forgiveness and eternal life. And He says, "Come and follow me." See, he shares his great victory with us. Can't earn it. Like a child, you simply trust, receive, and gladly submit yourself to Him. If you have never done that, then the promise of heaven does not right now apply to you. But today, if you hear my voice, God is calling out to you. He is offering you forgiveness, eternal life, a loving relationship with God, and real hope because of Jesus. Will you trust Him? We'll have pastors and others up here who would love to talk with you, pray with you, answer questions you may have.

Jesus Himself is our hope, even as we grieve on this awful day."

As I touched on before, I wanted three basic things from his service: strong message, good music and energy…

The music was especially important to me and it was easy to figure out what songs we would select and what message we wanted to be heard through them. I love just about any music I can understand the words to. I adore sweet harmonies and have a soft spot for the violin. I sang in our concert choir all through college and have since developed a love for powerful choral pieces. I miss the eight part harmonies.

Music has always been a part of my identity. For as long as I can remember, I was the guy who sings at things: church, weddings, funerals…whatever, really. I have performed at 94 weddings and 40 funerals to date…and cannot explain it to you, but just felt like I was supposed to sing at Grayden's, too. I was worried that people would think I was doing it to satisfy my own ego, but ultimately I was content in my motives.

As it turns out, five songs was not too many. The melodies were powerful, the messages direct. Complete with a congregational sing along and a choral benediction of nearly 40 voices, the music was exactly what we wanted it to be.

Jamie and I knew that the church would be filled with our family and friends, many of which struggled with issues of faith. We did not want anyone to leave the church following his services with the thought, "I don't want to serve a God who would kill a child." It was our hope that we could provide a celebration of our boy that would be filled with joy, energy and hope.

We felt a strong desire to "lead the charge" as we praised God through Grayden's services. A church full of bright shirts, balloons, a juggler, lots of music and hope was exactly what we were shooting for. To date, we have had over 20 people tell us they are going to start or re-start going to church as a result of those couple of days—and those are just the people who took the time to tell us that. That in itself can change generations of people…and I am proud to attach that to his legacy.

In a fitting end to an unexpectedly great day saw our family and friends release hundreds or red, yellow, green and blue balloons for our boy. The balloons were released at the same time and initially were all over the place. As they flew higher, it seemed as if they somehow magnetically clustered together and made their way directly to Grayden in heaven. People watched them float higher and there was a calm that accompanied the silence.

Had I not been there to see it myself, I am not sure I would've believed what happened next. In a somewhat surreal moment, it was as if God opened up the sky for the balloons to float directly into heaven…and they were seemingly gone—without a trace.

Wrote his eulogy

The day after he died, I sat down to write, and this is what was on the computer screen between 15 and 20 minutes later:

Grayden: Through the Eyes of Mommy and Daddy

It was truly our honor to get to be Grayden's mommy and daddy. From the moment we found out he would be joining our family, we loved him without hesitation.

We prayed for him for over a year before we learned he would be blessing our lives...and he never stopped doing that from that moment on.

If you never had the chance to spend any extended amount of time with him, please let us show you who our boy is through our eyes...

Grayden seemed to have the ability to light up a room when he entered. His smile was contagious and his dimples were simply too pronounced and perfect to overlook. He often carried himself with a sheepish grin, an ornery smile or eyes that would tell an entire story...and always, without a shadow of a doubt, his wrinkly eyebrows would be present to welcome you. Grayden seemed to have a magnetic ability to attract the attention of anyone who was close to him. He gave great hugs, was an exceptional zerbert-giver and could stop even the hardest of souls in their tracks with one single, "I love you."

Now, I know we are obviously biased, but Grayden was a pretty sharp young man. He counted past 20 and knew all of his shapes—with his favorite being the hexagon. We learned this when he requested his grilled cheese be cut into this...it seems the option of two rectangles, three triangles and four squares were simply not good enough. He also was as bilingual as a two year-old from a single language family in the Midwest could get. Once when asked how many cars he had, he responded by saying "TRES"...not sure it would've been believable had he not held up three cars to prove his point. And we would be remised if we did not mention his clever ability prolong the bedtime routine. A personal favorite had to be when he was heard yelling, "Daddy, I need you to come in to my room...pleeeeeeease daddy...I don't have any pants on...I mean it, daddy, come in right now, Swiper the Fox swiped them!"

Grayden seemed to function at a level far ahead of his years. He quoted his first movie at the age of two. We heard him yelling from the bathtub…"Daddy, I touched the butt, I touched the butt" Daddy, being a bit confused came into the bathroom to see him holding up his toy boat…and then he explained, "I touched the butt, daddy…just like Nemo."

He was focused on doing everything fast. He wanted to run fast, to kick fast and to spin fast.

He talked of his grandparents often and got excited every time there was a chance to talk to Grandma and Grandpa in Illinois. He loved Grandpa's train and always was ready for a ride on the big tractor. He loved to read books with Grandma, too. Grandma always played on the floor with him and they had a specific bedtime routine, complete with buttons and school bus books.

Grayden's Koko and Papa were two of his favorites as well. Grayden cooked with Koko and never missed an opportunity to rock with her. And unfortunately with our current string of unfortunate circumstances, Papa became "Mr. Fix-It." Anytime anything wasn't working, he would quickly say, "Papa fix it."

Grayden loved his little brother, Jayce. They played together every day…and Grayden, even though he got in a few legitimate shots, adored him. We constantly found ourselves saying, "Grayden, do not hug Jayce around the neck" and "Stop touching his face."

Grayden had many, many cousins that adored him as well…and he loved them all right back. He got so excited to see them that one time he even ran circles around the living room yelling, "thank you, thank you, thank you!"

We did everything we could to introduce him to Jesus. We talked about God openly, took Grayden to church on a regular basis and tried to explain why we pray and what purpose it served in our lives. Grayden became a serene little boy every time he heard us say, "It's time to say thank you to Jesus." He would stop what he was doing, fold his hands and prepare to listen.

Our favorite times were when we asked Grayden if he wanted to pray, and he said yes. His most memorable prayer went something like this: "Dear Jesus, um...I'm sorry I hit Jayce, um...and thank you for this food, Amen" And every time, without fail, Grayden would clap his hands and demand every person in the room do the same.

Our boy loved to be outside...and he played hard. Many times he would come back inside and his cheeks were flushed and his hair was damp with sweat...and he battled coming in, even though it was nearly dark and he could barely see.

Grayden had a soft spot for his shows: Dora, The Teenage Mutant

"Engine" Turtles, Bob the Builder, Thomas the Train, Bubble Guppies, Elmo's World and Team "Zoomi-zoomi." He was growing a fondness for Disney movies and loved Mickey Mouse.

Grayden got to spend three days a week with Miss Hannah...and we feel so fortunate he was able to learn how much she loved him while he was with us. Having Hannah in our home allowed for our boys to have some amazing advantages and we are truly grateful for her presence in our lives.

We loved hugging Grayden because he was truly good at it. Best part about it was his hugs were often accompanied by a sincere and heartfelt question. Namely, "Are you happy, mommy?" and "Do I make you happy, Daddy?" We take so much joy from knowing that he understood these feelings. He knew we loved him because we verbalized it to him on a regular basis. We consistently asked him, "Who loves you?" and he would rattle off a list of at least 8 names— Mommy and Daddy and Jayce were always first, and we adore that. And when we turned the tables and asked him who he loved, he always started his list by saying some combination of the same three names.

Our hearts are broken at the earthly loss of our young hero. And under normal circumstances, this formalized "goodbye" would be something that we could not comprehend. Instead, we choose to alter the words just a bit. Our goodbye, becomes, "we cannot wait to join you in heaven, our sweet and precious boy."

Mommy and daddy love you very much but we know that we took advantage of our opportunity to tell you about Jesus. Now, Grayden, heaven's newest and handsomest little hero, it is Jesus' turn to tell you about us. We know you will enjoy learning up there as much as you did here.

We offer you to God with absolutely no regrets because mommy loved you "to pieces, to pieces, to pieces" and daddy consistently gave you "kisses, kisses, kisses, kisses, kisses."

Go now and be with Jesus and never hurt again. Be in your perfect, fever-free body and know that Mommy and Daddy will be along soon to join you.

When I read this to Jamie, we made one minor change. It was exactly what I wanted it to be.

"Grayden turning into Superman" might be my favorite picture of him. This is a lasting image of our little "Man of Steele"

I can usually say whatever I want when I write—but it often takes a bit. Talking about Grayden proved to be no challenge at all. The words came to me quickly and in less than 20 minutes, I had completed my most treasured written piece. One might think that title would've gone to one of the many papers I wrote in my 23 years of schooling – four of which I studied journalism, but that is not the case. Being able to tell the world about my boy, and our love and adoration for him trumped everything else I had ever created with a typewriter or computer…and it wasn't even close.

Cried...a lot

There was one constant in our first year: sadness.

Sadness was the one thing I experienced every day. Recognizing emotion and letting it happen is not something I struggle with. I am not afraid to cry, I don't have an issue laughing out loud and when I get frustrated, people generally know this. Point is, I am not scared to feel—and I am not ashamed to let others see this.

I can honestly say I encountered sadness every day. It didn't always last long, but it often did. It didn't consume me every time, but sometimes it did. The common denominator in all of this is that each of these responses was okay.

The worst part for me was trying to understand and make sense of what had happened...and what was continuing to happen. Our world was rapidly changing and it was not a change I wanted to entertain. I missed him on a regular basis and that was not an easy thing to feel.

I found myself in the presence of tears for many different reasons:

I cried when I was sad

I cried when I missed him

I cried when I was happy—because he didn't get to experience the happiness

I cried when I thought about the future

I cried when I couldn't sleep

I cried when I watched videos of him

I cried when I couldn't stop thinking

You sensing a trend here?

There was a period of about a month when I couldn't feel…and I didn't trust it so I worked hard to move past it. Feeling is important, even if you are not sure of what kind of day you are experiencing. I had a ton of days like this…and I have now learned to embrace them.

In September, exactly 8 months after we lost him, this is the kind of day I was having:

"Here is what I am thinking today…

I miss my boy on a regular basis. There are things that make me miss him more every time I see them or think about them, (baseball, fishing, giving him the keys to the car, math homework, teaching him how to treat women) and others that sneak up on me--and I never know what those moments are going to be.

Today, I went to see the Cardinals beat the Cubs…and I thought of him a lot. Maybe it was because the only game he got to go to was a Cardinal victory over the Cubs…maybe it was because I realized he'd never be able to do some of the things I was seeing…maybe that is just going to be my normal--who knows…and it doesn't really matter.

I saw kids everywhere smiling, laughing and loving life…and it made me feel close to him and broke my heart again all at the same time.

Today was a gathering of people that supported children with Down Syndrome… and I have always had a heart for that…I saw some amazing smiles from kids who were not afraid to smile big…I saw a girl give Fredbird the biggest hug I have ever seen and it made me happy--even though I cried. I saw families love their children and it made me fell close to him and break my heart all over again.

And even though I found myself fighting tears all day, I would trade today for nothing.

I wanted him to love life and not be afraid to smile big and experience emotion… regardless of what it looked like…and I believe he did.

As today winds down, I think of Grayden and am so glad he is walking with Jesus. If I close my eyes I can see him playing catch with the angels and fishing with the people who love him that have already gone home.

I cannot wait to see him again and know that because of Jesus that I will experience that. In the meantime, it is God's plan for me to be here...and I am grateful for that opportunity.

I have come to terms with the fact that random waves of emotion will be my normal...and I have accepted this. I invite you to laugh and cry with me. I don't know about you, but in order for me to be me and achieve the things I want to achieve, I have to be emotional. That means I will laugh out loud--even when it might be awkward and ill-timed. I will embrace my belly laugh and try to get you to use yours more often.

I will cry hard and tear up when I don't expect to...and then I will break the silence because I hate it...seriously, silence is creepy to me.

I will react strongly when someone is wronged...and if you bring up something that annoys me, I might go on a 3-5 minute tangent in which I am completely fired up.

I will react too strongly, recognize I am wrong and ask for forgiveness.

I will do some of these things at the same time and it will be confusing, profound, frustrating and amazing all at the same time...but to different people.

I will praise God for my life and my family...and for Grayden. I will praise Him for taking Grayden home before I wanted him to go. I will praise Him because he took him home...that is what i wanted for my boy.

How could I be a good father to him if I didn't. I wanted Grayden to experience heaven and am not one to challenge God because I don't understand his timing.

I will continue to miss him...because I don't know how to do it any other way--and I will be okay with that because that is my normal.

And through all of this, I will remember that my wife and child are still here and need me...and I will revel in that role and give them my all.

I will do this because it is how it should be and they deserve it...and all the while I will remember that life on earth (although I will certainly never take it for granted) is just a short time when compared to eternity.

In the long run, our time away will be very short...and that is pretty amazing.

So tomorrow I will wake up and be psyched about the prospects of a new day...I will go praise God--sing about him, listen to his word and worship him...even though I will probably want to sleep some more instead. Then I will come home and put on my Grayden #25 Bears jersey and watch the Bears game because it is on TV... before I take a nap...then I will watch more football and check the score to see the if the Redbirds beat the lowly Cubs again and have secured home field advantage in the playoffs, probably be upset with my fantasy team and play with Jayce...and it will be a great day--there is even cold pizza in the fridge for breakfast...(cold chicken would be better)."

I have learned there are no right or wrong days…days are just what they are. I am finally okay with letting them be just that.

Disliked my wife
for almost 3 months

This is not something I am proud of, but that does not mean it isn't reality. To say we hit a rough patch is an understatement. Our pain was so real and consumed us to the level that we shut down on each other.

What we found out was that not only were we dealing with things in completely different manners (which has to be acceptable) but that we got to a point where we simply did not care what the other was feeling.

By not talking to each other and making an effort to weather through this together, we cemented a wedge that many couples cannot overcome. We were fortunate that we did not let this get the best of us.

It is not a period of time I enjoyed, but is, nonetheless, still a vivid picture in my head. We were consistently entertaining thoughts of frustration, anger and irritation. We seldom talked, except to attack each other and defend ourselves.

It was horrible.

I think we shrugged it off believing it was an appropriate response to what had happened in our lives, but I cannot be okay with believing that to be truth. Let me explain:

I know it would be naïve for us to assume things would be easy—and not one time did we believe that to be the case. But to expect this to happen and to be okay with it citing it as a normal reaction is not okay either. This happened to us, not because we lost our little boy, but because we allowed it to happen. No excuses, no justifications—we did this to ourselves. Once we got on the same page, we realized we weren't really that far apart after all. We wanted the same things for ourselves and for each other. We just got stuck in recognizing how that could be achieved. Our own personal desires took control of our decision-making and our motivations. The result was a horrid stretch that I feel content saying neither of us ever want to experience again.

Why do I mention this? It is certainly not because I enjoy my own personal gossip. It is because we were lucky enough to fight through this, with the help of our grief counselor. Together, we overcame a huge obstacle to accomplish our goal of unity. We did what needed to happen to give ourselves a shot to succeed again. Simply put, we were one of the lucky ones who realized this before it was too late.

I share this not because I want to highlight our pain to embarrass myself or any member of our family. I share this because vulnerability in situations like this provides reality. If people want to understand how this really works, they cannot just view the good times when things aren't as bad as they once were. They need to see the raw moments in which pain consumes a family. After all, pain in this situation is commonplace.

One of our first pictures
together—still one of
my favorites

Recorded the songs
from his funeral

Shortly after his services, we were moved by the amount of people who seemed to find a connection with the music from Grayden's funeral.

We truly believed we picked the right songs to communicate what we wanted them to communicate. We received several requests to publish the titles of the songs that were performed. We also received numerous requests that people wanted copies of the songs.

Prepping the music for his service was like nothing else I have ever been a part of.

Our friend, Russ, is the worship leader at one of the five locations of our church, was the first person we talked to. We contacted him to see if he would be able to help us out and luckily, he was able and willing. We gave him a list of songs, "What Do I Know of Holy" by Addison Road, "Praise You in This Storm" by Casting Crowns, Chris Rice's "Go Light Your World," "Jesus Paid it All," and my favorite choral piece, "In The Upper Room" and the ball was rolling. He contacted the worship leader from our church, David, and we had a group of three people ready to perform for God, and for Grayden.

I was nervous about the process—on multiple levels. First and foremost, I didn't know if I would be able to sing these songs without becoming too emotional. However, I knew I had to try.

Also, although I am confident in my vocal abilities, I have never truly considered myself a musician as I do not play an instrument. I would soon be in the presence of gifted musicians and I was both humbled and excited to have them be a part of this. I didn't know what that really meant until our rehearsal.

We were slated to meet at the church and as I parked, I took a brief minute to pray. My prayer was direct and compact, "Dear Lord, please allow me to be able to perform these songs tomorrow."

From there, I walked into the sanctuary and found Russ and David ready to go. I had lyric sheets printed out and also had looked on iTunes and knew we would be able to order background tracks if necessary.

My first conversation with the guys went something like this, "Okay, so we can order tracks if we need to…"

I was quickly cut off by Russ, "Dude, We are not using any tracks…don't worry, we are going to make this happen."

I believed him and I was thrilled. I love the acoustic sound and had no idea how pleased I would be with what we were able to create.

Of the four songs Jamie and I had selected, Russ and David each knew one—and it was not the same song. To me, this seemed an unrealistic task. However, 40 minutes after we started our rehearsal, we had performance ready versions of each song ready to go. It was amazing and at that moment I knew I was going to be able to sing each song…cannot explain why, God just provided me with a sense of calm I trusted.

Each of those songs touched on an important idea we wanted to be highlighted through his funeral. It was our hope that the music would speak to those in attendance as much as it did us. I, for one, believe we were able to do that.

Perhaps the most important song for me was "In The Upper Room." Its importance to me, and to our family, begins my freshman year of college—that was the first time I heard it, and performed it.

Every year, our choir took a weeklong tour. During my four years, we visited Nashville, Atlanta, Kansas City and Dallas. We gave an average of 10-14 performances and each evening concert, usually at a church, was concluded with 60 voices surrounding the outside of the church and singing this particular piece. Its piano part is sweet, its harmonies will give you chills and its message will provide you hope.

I loved it so much, that I put a choir together to sing it at our wedding. It was my gift to Jamie and it was perfect.

Additionally, I sang it to each of my boys as a lullaby. They know the tune and I believed when Grayden heard it, from his perfect seat in heaven, that he would be comforted in its familiarity and beauty.

I contacted some friends from college, along with other musical friends and we soon had a choir of about 40 voices to perform Grayden a final lullaby. I cannot think of a more appropriate benediction to conclude his service.

Knowing what this music meant to me and seeing that others had requested copies as well, Jamie gave me the perfect birthday gift—some studio time to lay the tracks from that day.

Our little rock star at two years old

I contacted Russ and David again and we were able to get some time lined up to get back together to re-create the music from that day. In lieu of going to the recording studio, we opted to go to our church's main campus and perform each track live. We decided not only would it save some cost, but it would also recreate the original feel from that day.

The end result was a product I am proud of. It glorifies God and is a lasting memory for us, our family and our friends.

The significance of this is simple, I don't want to be afraid to relive that day. I don't want that day to haunt me and having a lasting memory from that day that is a source of pride is important to the healing process. It was our goal to provide people with hope and comfort in a horrible time. I believe we were able to accomplish that on some level for various members of our family and friends. I am sure of one thing, I am positive we were able to do that for me.

Went to a benefit
for our family

I had a migraine that lasted seven weeks. During that time, I lost 50 pounds, some of my sanity and self-worth and my job. I spent two weeks at Mayo clinic and ended up having heart surgery. We came back from Christmas and our furnace quit…and we had some plumbing issues in the only shower in our house. The check engine lights clicked on in both of our vehicles. At this point, we thought things could not get any worse and we joked about what might happen next—because it was easier than being constantly upset.

And then Grayden died.

We knew God was prepping us for something, we just had no idea it was this.

Our family was broken, my health was not getting any better and finances were an issue. I was able to transition to disability through my work but we were only able to recover two thirds of my salary. Don't get me wrong, I am grateful to have that security, but with Jamie only working part-time, it put us in a bit of a bind.

That was when we got the phone call.

On the other end was my sister-in-law Kari and our friend Paul. Paul is a classically trained musician with a heart to help. On a conference phone call, they informed us that they were planning a benefit for us.

It would be a concert with Paul and three other vocalists, two of which were friends of Jamie. Additionally, Paul's wife, Martha, a classically trained cellist, was putting together a string quintet that would be performing music she scored.

Overwhelmed, grateful and unsure how to respond, they asked our permission to proceed and we fought back tears as we thanked them and told them, "yes."

You want to talk about a humbling experience? Go to a benefit for yourself.

We talked about how to handle the day of the event. Should we go? Is that even appropriate?

We talked to Paul and Kari and they both encouraged us to attend. The outpouring of support was massive and immense. Numerous people donated auction and raffle items and the music was phenomenal.

It was an emotional day on many levels.

The money raised gave us some breathing room and took an enormous amount of pressure off of us.

Within a couple months after the benefit, Jamie was able to secure full-time employment and our situation took a turn for the better.

This benefit was one of many amazing acts of kindness we received in the year after we lost him. Our friends and family were always present and our support system truly revealed itself as a constant source of strength.

It was difficult to see people want to help us because I considered it my responsibility to provide for my family financially. However, when I was physically unable to do that, I learned to check my pride, ask for help and humbly receive it—whether I liked it or not.

Wrote a children's book

It actually became more of a poem. My intent was to write a book that flows well and would speak to children. I wanted to talk about death and make it not seem so scary and so unfamiliar. I was not able accomplish that in my first attempt:

This is Grayden, he is two and he's a special boy

He loves his family, they love him, they brought each other joy

Grayden likes to watch his shows and loves his brother Jayce

He loves to build and play with trucks, and really likes to race

His favorite is to be outside, he loves his backyard toys

He always welcomes time with "friends," the other girls and boys

His smile is huge, his dimples too, he gives the best darn hugs

He has a way of finding how, he grabs your heart and tugs

But this is where the story turns, our hearts are broken hence

We find that we will shift to speaking of him in past tense

Grayden went to take a nap, a healthy two year old

And woke up in the arms of God, within the streets of gold

He didn't hurt, there was no pain, he simply closed his eyes

And woke up in the best of care in need of no goodbyes

We know that we will see him soon, that certainly will be

And now we move ahead on earth a family of three

We say this with a heavy heart and know we'll not forget

We're thankful for the view he has from where he now must sit

There will be days when it is hard, I'm sure there'll be a few

We'll do our best to give ourselves, completely back to You

We ask for You to heal us and we look to You for hope

We know that in You lies the best chance that we have to cope

And when it hurts and we lose sight and cannot find our way

We ask that you will hold us then and guide us through the day

Send us those reminders that will gently ease our pain

Help us all to recognize the things we all will gain

One thing that we will not forget, reminding of His love

The moon is round, we do know this, for this we're thankful of

Yet on those days when you lose track of what can bring you calm

Remember that the moon is round, and we must carry on

This is a simple note of faith, reminding more than me

God is there just like the moon, no matter what we see

To all of those who mourn with us, we share our hearts and tears

We're thankful that you knew our boy and hope to ease your fears

So close your eyes and go to sleep and do not fear the worst

Grayden's where he wants to be, he got to go there first

In this we mourn and miss our boy and look to what comes now

We know that with the help of God, that we will figure how

Until the day we see him there in heaven's perfect place

We memorize the little things we loved about his face

His laugh was great, he showed us love, he changed us from the start

We never dreamed we'd have to learn our lives with him apart

Forget is not an option and we know we'll see you soon

For now I'll think of my big boy each time I see the moon

So go with God and learn about the perfect place you are

And save a spot for each of us, our bright and shining star

We cannot wait to see you and your thought will never fade

We're thankful for the memories on earth that you have made

As you look down, you'll know for sure we gave you all our love

We cannot wait to share with you the same from up above

We love you and we'll miss you, that is certainly for real

You changed us for the better, precious hero, Grayden Steele

I wrote that a week after he died. And while it is not the book I'd hoped to read to Jayce one day to help answer some of his questions, I think there is a place for it. This is a prime illustration of the role coping skills play in moving on. Writing has often served as medicine for me and this time it was no different. This was a necessary outlet for me when I wanted to shut down. Looking back, I wish I had done this more often.

Invited our friends' kids over and made a snow slide

Here is what the invite looked like:

"Snow party in our backyard tomorrow...please bring your kids and play with us. Snowmen, snow angels and hot chocolate for sure. Disney movies and cupcakes for the thaw afterwards.

Grayden only got to play in the snow twice because we just never had enough snow when he was here. (And he never saw snow like this when he was old enough to walk!)

Help us use our backyard to honor him and have some kid-friendly fun in the process. I want to make a giant snowman...maybe two or three--and this snow is great for that!!!

Let me know if you are in...anytime works for me."

I was so excited...it was late March and we really got dumped on. An unexpected surprise—especially considering we didn't have a significant snowfall the previous winter. I wanted our backyard to be filled with bodies, laughter and joy...and I got my wish.

As the day was winding down, my excitement became bittersweet. I was still looking forward to the "snow party" but all of a sudden was missing Grayden terribly.

I found the following journal entry:

"Missing my boy...looking forward to playing in the snow tomorrow. I love that he has a great seat to watch us, but hate that he is not here to take part. He would've been all over this..."

What happened the following day was something I could never have predicted.

We had twelve friends show up...and the kids (and adults) had a blast. Midway through the morning, our friend Paul started packing the snow in an attempt to construct a makeshift hill for sledding. The snow was perfect for packing and made the hill come together quickly.

I grabbed some shovels and buckets and we started building. An hour later, the slide was over twelve feet from the ground and over 60 feet long.

The day was topped off with some warm cookies and hot chocolate.

A perfect tribute to our boy. A great way to remember him and have fun in the process. I look forward to doing it again soon.

The view from the top. This is toward the end of construction.

All in all, more than 20 people went down the slide that day.

Took our friends to the hospital following their miscarriage

It was exactly one month after we lost Grayden. I hated the 28th for about 5 months before I realized it was silly to blame heartache on a number.

We cried for and with them…and met their daughter who only made it to 16 weeks in her mother's womb.

I hate that we had to share pain with them. I understood the helpless feeling everyone around us must've felt. I wanted to fix it and eliminate their pain… instead, I sat with them, listened and cried alongside them.

An original painting
inspired by the funeral

Went to a weekend retreat for couples who have lost a young child

We got an e-mail from our pastor with some information about Respite Retreat, a weekend retreat for couples who've lost a young child. It would include 10-12 couples and was put on by Nancy and David Guthrie, who had lost two children themselves.

In reading his e-mail, his message was simple: "I think you should consider this."

He went on to offer financial support from the church and said the idea originated when he was reaching out to peers in an effort to try to find support for couples in our situation. To compound this, there was another couple in our church family who'd also lost their daughter. I am grateful that he took the initiative to seek out some aid for us.

After doing our research, we were excited to be heading to Nashville. I don't think either of us expected the weekend to be as amazing as it was for us, though.

We'd lost Grayden a month and a half before and knew we needed all the help we could get. What we got was a weekend without guilt, support from people who were going through the same things and some lifelong friends and confidantes.

Of the twelve couples, including the leaders, 14 children were lost. The stories differed in specifics but were identical in result: each of us not only lost our child, but also our ability understand normal.

We cried that weekend with new people. We shared stories and swapped hypotheticals...and everyone understood. There was no worrying about perception. There was no needing to explain our thoughts or motivations. There was no guilt in laughing and feeling like ourselves again because people there knew what it was like.

We shared stories and found similarities. We processed through what worked and didn't work for each of us. We listened and found hope in our truth.

That weekend I felt like I got to know 13 other children that I will not meet until I get to heaven.

There is something soothing about believing I will recognize them once I get there. Their stories were all unique and their faces are engrained in my mind. I believe Grayden plays regularly in heaven with Samuel, Sadie, Gwen, Molly, Charlie, Hope, Gabe, Gabriel, Ava, Caleb, Henryk and Leah.

Their bodies are all perfect and they live without flaw. They run, they sing, they dance…they have their mother's eyes and their father's spirit. There is no pain. There is no discomfort. There is no struggle.

Grayden's new friends in heaven

Won a trivia night
for Grayden

Our friend Jason, who was a groomsman in our wedding, pulled me aside at the funeral and said he wanted to be able to do something for us. He said he'd been thinking and he wanted to host a trivia night at the college we both attended and that I had worked at just a couple years before. He said there were a ton of people who wanted to help but needed an outlet and he wanted to provide that for us.

Jason knew I loved trivia and thought it would be a fitting way to pay tribute to Grayden and raise some money to help our family…and he was right.

We saw some of my former classmates, fraternity brothers and colleagues. There were current college students present that wanted to support the cause. My parents, my niece and my nephew made the trip to see us as well.

Grayden rocking the monkey pajamas at Grandma and Grandpas

That night we had fun, we enjoyed ourselves for a bit. We gave and received hugs and shared an evening with our friends. And…we won!

Jason's gift to us was appreciated like he will never know. I was, and am, proud to be his friend. The event more than tripled his goal, and our family benefitted from it directly.

In perhaps what was my favorite part of the evening, my niece came up to me shortly before the start of the first round and said, "Uncle Brent, I want you to have this." She gave me an envelope with two five dollar bills and ten ones inside. I looked at her a bit confused and she said to me, "It is money I made babysitting and I want you to have it for the trivia night."

I tried to refuse to take it encouraging her to save her money and was quickly re-directed. "Uncle Brent, please. I want you to have this. I brought it here for you."

With that, I accepted my 12 year old niece's generosity and beamed with pride at the young woman she was becoming. Her heart was so good and I wept at her selflessness in that moment.

It was a great evening, a reminder of the importance of friendship and family. An opportunity to give and receive hugs—to give and receive love. We cried both happy and sad tears that night, and I loved every minute of it.

Bought my wife a personalized Cardinals jersey

Jamie and I are big St. Louis Cardinals fans and have been fortunate enough to be able to go to a fair amount of games through the years. I'd always wanted to get Jamie a jersey but didn't know which route to go. Her favorite player was David Eckstein, but he was no longer with the team. When we lost Grayden, I had what I thought was the perfect jersey idea for her.

I shopped around for a plain cardinals jersey in a women's cut. The best deal I found was from a Chinese company and the savings was sizeable enough that I decided to give it a shot.

My plan was to have custom lettering put on the jersey that read:

G. Steele

2.5

I had called around to find a place that would do the lettering and was all set.

I did run into a little bit of a snag, though. Prior to having the custom lettering completed, I wanted to make sure the jersey fit like Jamie wanted it to. So, I wrapped it and gave it to her for Christmas. I told her my plan and asked her to try it on…and it fit!

After some discussion, she found the courage to tell me, "I think I would want Grayden Steele on it, is that okay?" She went on to say she really loved his name so I was content to change my plan. What happened next was one of my favorite parts of that Christmas season.

Jayce and I drove around the parking lot of our local mall for about 45 minutes before we lucked out and found a spot. I went directly to the sporting goods store I knew did custom lettering and explained to them what I was hoping for. That is when it happened…

If it were up to me, Santa's sleigh would've flown by itself this year. I would like to thank the "Santa" employee at the sporting goods store for his heart and compassion.

After I told him of the special circumstances of the job...double name and decimal point in the number, I could see the wheels turning and he was figuring out a way to make this gift for Jamie perfect.

When I went to pay for the custom lettering, I was told, "You don't have to pay for that, sir...we want to take care of this for you."

With tears in my eyes, I turned to thank him and he told me to thank the gentleman working on the jersey, because it was "his call."

When I went over to speak to him, he was lining everything out with tears in his eyes. I grabbed his attention to thank him and he was unable to speak.

When he was finished, he looked around the store until he found Jayce and me. He held the jersey up with pride in his smile and tears sliding down his cheeks.

He brought me the jersey, gave me a big hug and said, "Merry Christmas, Sir."

Thank you, young man...you have earned my business any time I have sporting goods needs...but more importantly, you renewed my faith and strengthened my Christmas spirit. God bless you!

Started anti-anxiety medication

The truth is, I got to the point where I was unable to manage it on my own.

I started medication to help take the edge off. I was unable to sleep and struggled with every noise I heard—believing it was Jayce having a seizure. It became a compulsion and it was spinning out of control.

I spoke with my doctor and we started a low dose anti-anxiety medication with some anti-depressive characteristics hoping to potentially kill two birds with one stone. I really seemed to benefit early on but after a short time, I felt like I wasn't able to "feel" at all. I really felt like I was shut down emotionally. Not only did that not feel like me, but I did not like it and it was necessary to make a change.

With the assistance of my doctor, I switched medicines with success. We started at a low dose and later increased to a level that was extremely effective for me.

Do I like that I needed medication? Nope. But I believe I needed it. This will probably not be a long-term thing, but I will not be afraid to take it if I need it. My goal is simple: be me again, enjoy life and take care of my family.

I recognized it was even more confusing to try to establish a new normal when I didn't really feel like myself at all. Once I got to where I could function on a more normal and consistent level, it was easier for me to take better care of my family.

Went to grief counseling with my wife

And it saved our marriage.

We'd forgotten how to talk to each other and were content with going through the motions…which made us despise each other on some level. Our lives had become about pain, sadness, frustration and irritation. Through our counseling, we found ourselves again—both individually and as a couple.

Our situation had become bigger than us…and we needed help. I am thankful we sought and received it.

Attended a former student's wedding

I have been fortunate enough to remain close with many of my students after their graduations. That seems to be one of the many perks of working at, and attending a small, private college. I knew almost everyone on campus, and knew a lot of them well.

My second year as the Director of Student Activities at Culver-Stockton College, we introduced a new philanthropy to campus. Up 'Til Dawn was a fundraising effort for St. Jude's Children's Research Hospital. The program was supported through ALSAC, St. Jude's fundraising arm.

We took on the challenge and tried to raise as much money as we could.

Our response was truly astounding. St. Jude's goal for us was to have 12 teams, and we had 42. St. Jude's goal for us was to raise $10,000-12,000 and we raised over $42,000. That's right, a student population of 800 raised over forty-two grand in one night.

One of my students who served as co-director of the student group responsible for the event was Sam. I advised the group and worked closely with Sam and our other co-director, Jessi. That was the single most important accomplishment of my professional career and I think it had a similar effect on my students as well.

Nearly four years later, I got Sam's wedding invitation in the mail. Jamie and I were extremely excited that we would get to attend.

I hadn't seen Sam since we lost Grayden. She was unable to make it down for services because of a hectic work schedule and I knew she struggled with that. Similar things had happened with the large group of students that I suspected would be at the wedding. We knew they all wanted to attend, but were just not able to make it happen.

As we prepped for the wedding, we were eager to see everyone but nervous about how we would respond as well. We gave and received a lot of hugs and it was a great weekend. I adore that crew of students that were there and we talked a lot about Grayden. It meant the world to us that they wanted to know how we were doing and to see them listen intently as I told stories about my boy. They laughed hard and cried softly as I sincerely believe they got to know him a bit more.

Selfishly, my favorite part of the weekend was when I finally got to see Sam at the reception. She noticed me from across the room and threw her arms in the air and ran over to see me, tears in her eyes.

I remember her yelling out through the tears "Brent and Jamie are here…yea, I am so excited. I love you guys so much and I think about you every day."

It warmed my heart that on the most important day of her life, our pain was still close to her heart.

I told her, "I am struggling with the fact that I am finding joy in a bride crying to see me on her wedding day." Sam smiled and said, "It's going to be okay, I am so glad you are here."

And I knew she was right—I knew we were going to be okay.

Hosted a game
night at our house

Just like old times…just like we did when he was here. Just like when before our days were consistently difficult.

We had fun and felt normal again.

I don't even remember if my team won--and it didn't matter.

A photo from the first annual
board game decathlon

Missed him

This happened every day…multiple times a day. It comes and goes in duration and intensity.

I don't expect that to ever change--and to be honest, I don't want to not miss him. (I would be okay if the intensity lessened, though.)

I expect him to be a part of my thought process on a regular basis. Missing him is not a bad thing…it is not something that will haunt me. Instead, it will allow me to love him and be motivated to live my life in a manner that would make him proud that I am his dad.

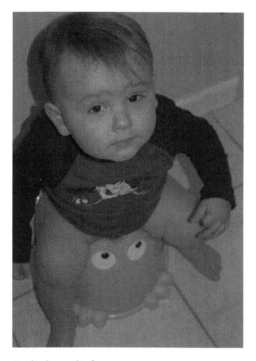

Our big boy on his frog potty

Decorated for Christmas

One of the first things I worried about was whether or not I should put up his stocking at Christmastime. I was worrying about this in February—that should show you how "all over the place" my thought process was.

Christmas has always been my favorite. I love the lights, the music and the energy. Christmas makes me think of family, traditions and love—and those are all feelings I welcome.

For as long as I can remember, I have loved stockings the best. I love gifts with a purpose and that tell a story.

Every year we would get an ornament in our stocking. We would get two packs of Trident gum…and I would always get one package of cinnamon and one package of either blue or green gum. I hate cinnamon gum so I traded it immediately with my sister, Anita.

At grandma's we always got an orange and a snickers bar…and each year the mystery of the Christmas stocking was "to what fast food restaurant would our $5 of gift certificates be to?"

The first year we didn't have stockings I was inappropriately upset…as I was old enough to know better.

With that being known, I guess I should not be surprised that I worried about his stocking.

I wanted to do the right thing for our family. I didn't want to put it up and have it be a reminder of pain. I didn't want our home to become a shrine to him and I had no idea whether or not it was appropriate to hang his stocking up when he was spending Christmas with God and not with us.

So much of what I was afraid of revolved around saving myself or my family from pain…and so many of the decisions I was facing did not have a clear-cut answer. There was no guidebook to follow and I found I was going to have to make these decisions myself and deal with the consequences.

My issue was not complex, but it wasn't simple either.

I talked about my struggle with the stocking to anyone who would listen. I was scared to do the wrong thing—scared someone would perceive it was the wrong move.

I worried about how I would feel when I pulled it out of the box it was stored in. I worried about Jamie's response.

I made the decision long before it was time to decorate, that his stocking would be hung because he is a member of our family...and it was the right call for us.

When December rolled around and I was looking at our fifteen plus boxes of Christmas decorations, the season took over and fear was nowhere in sight. I was overwhelmed, not with sadness or grief, but with the spirit of Christmas.

When I hung his stocking in line with the rest of ours, it felt right. I didn't even catch myself breathing funny. When I see them hanging I am reminded that we are a family of four...and at least for a brief moment, it doesn't feel broken. It doesn't feel incomplete and it doesn't matter that one of us is in heaven.

I did, however, have a problem seeing it hanging by itself Christmas morning when we took ours down. As a matter of fact, I hated it—it broke my heart.

I think I have come up with an easy fix...at least in theory.

Every year, we will fill his stocking. When we take down our stockings to partake in Christmas morning festivities, we will take his down with ours.

After the holidays, we will find some charitable organization to donate the contents to. It will be our hope that it will bring joy to another child in Grayden's memory.

Ideally, we would do this before the season so they could find their way to a toys for tots program. However, selfishly, I am not ready for that yet...maybe we will shoot for that in year three.

Went back to the church his funeral service was held in

It was inevitable. That church was our home. We will forever be connected to it because it was the site of the most significant event in each of our lives.

Was I nervous to return there? Nope—at least not until after I was already there.

I realized that the last time I saw him, he was in this room. He was lying peacefully and quietly and it didn't seem real, even though I knew it was.

I found myself going to sit in the sanctuary just to be. I liked the quiet-which was a switch for me. I liked the connection I felt to Christ and indirectly, to Grayden.

This was the last place I kissed him…it was where I told him it was okay for him to go, where I promised him we'd be along soon.

That room does not haunt me. Instead, it grounds me and has become a safe place. I don't think there is any coincidence in that.

Ordered his tombstone

I don't think I am being over-emotional or dramatic when I say no parents ever want to pick out their child's tombstone—I know I sure did not.

However, we had to do this for our boy.

We learned that there are a lot of options...and that different cemeteries have certain stipulations as well.

I initially looked at this as the last thing I could do *right* for him. I knew that there would be people whose only introduction to Grayden would be his grave marker...and I wanted it to be perfect...I wanted it to do him justice.

We picked out a dark stone and added a picture. The cemetery mandated that there be a religious symbol on the stone and we selected a classic cross.

At this point, that hard part was done. Now we'd have to wait and see how we responded when we first saw the stone.

I worried that this would somehow make things feel final—but prior to seeing the stone in place, I came to terms with the fact that *this* was already final.

I missed my boy and he was not coming back.

With this realization, the stone was transformed from a final opportunity into natural next step.

I want the stone to look sharp and represent him well. However, I have plenty of opportunities to do things right in his name.

Organized a trivia night to help fund the completion of his memorial playground

Gifts to Grayden's memorial raised about $6,000 for the playground project. We were overwhelmed with support.

As we crunched the numbers, we knew we could put together a good playground with the amount of money we raised. But, I was driven to create an amazing playground which meant we would need more funds.

I approached leadership at our church about the possibility of raising the rest of the money and received the go ahead.

Working in student activities and event planning, I had a few ideas about how to best raise these funds. After some deliberation, we opted to go with a trivia night.

We would secure a location, do some publicity and create an event that would hopefully be supported by the members of our church.

Our congregation is young and would benefit directly from this so it was our hope that we could provide an outlet for a cause our church family would rally behind.

My favorite part about the prep for this event was the selection of questions. I had decided to write them myself, which would allow me to tailor them however I would like.

I decided to go the pop culture route: movies, television, current events, sports and music. I thought it would speak to our target audience and make for a fun evening.

What I liked even more was the opportunity to highlight Grayden through these questions.

I could pay tribute to him by writing questions in categories that represented him: his likes, his stories, his memories.

Obviously 100 about a 2 and a half year old would be difficult to make work for an adult audience, so I had to be creative. I added subcategories. For instance Grayden loved Mickey Mouse so the first category was *Mickey Mouse: Famous Mickeys or Mice.*

In emceeing the event, I can share stories of our boy and make connections that will make the event more personal.

The event has yet to happen, but the questions are written and we are waiting for the right time.

The entire playground project was a good thing for me. It gave me something positive to focus on when I struggled to find those outlets on my own. Part of the key to being able to successfully move on is finding things to believe in again.

Set his memorials to benefit the Dravet Syndrome Foundation and to build a playground at our church

Grayden did not have Dravet Syndrome, a rare type of epilepsy that begins in infancy. We do believe however, without having the results of the autopsy, that his death was caused or at least influenced by a seizure. Grayden had febrile (fever induced) seizures when he got sick and based on how we found him, we believe this to be the case. The way the doctors explained it to us, his fever came on so fast and his body's natural defense was to fight it. Unfortunately, the way his body fought the fever led to a neural misfire that resulted in a seizure. This is not uncommon in children and we were repeatedly told it "was not dangerous, it was just scary to watch." We still believe this to be this case...we are chalking this up to an unfortunate fluke. Grayden met with two separate neurologists and had an EEG to check his brain. The EEG came back completely normal and they assured us he did not have a seizure disorder.

One of Jamie's best friends' sons has Dravet Syndrome and we have become supporters of fundraising for the Dravet Syndrome Foundation through them. We thought this was an amazing opportunity to raise awareness in Grayden's honor to help boys and girls like Finn. In addition to fighting Dravet Syndrome, the Dravet Syndrome Foundation provides resources to all families whose children have seizures. This seemed to be an appropriate choice for a memorial.

Our second choice for a memorial is the Journey Kids program at The Journey - Hanley Road Campus. Every week Grayden got excited to go to church to be with his friends. Journey Kids is a volunteer driven, childcare program for the youth of our church's congregation.

More specifically, we will use memorial funds to construct a playground. Our church is full of young couples and children. However, our playground does not do our population justice.

I contacted one of my best friends from high school who is an architect. He owns his own business with his wife, a landscape architect. They were thrilled to be a part of the project and donated their time to make it happen. We met with them and they looked at the space...what they came up with was perfect.

Once the renderings were complete and the plan was in place, we finalized the equipment needed to complete the project. We found a playground supply store about 15 miles from our house that was touched by Grayden's story. They offered to sell us all of our equipment at an extremely discounted rate, much of it at their cost.

This project became very personal to me. I love the message it sends and the outlets it provides for families. I look forward to watching numerous children, Grayden's friends, enjoy this structure for years to come.

Attended and took part in a Superhero 5K run

Jamie found a Super Hero 5K to benefit an anti-bullying and suicide prevention organization and we were excited to participate. We were attracted to it initially because of the super hero theme, but were pleased to be able to support what we think is a good cause in the process.

We dressed Jayce up in his Spider-Man Halloween costume and Jamie and I wore the capes our students made us for Grayden's funeral over top of our Superman shirts.

I had purchased some super hero fabric and expanded upon the capes. They were red with a gold "G" painted in the middle. Only now the original red cape was framed with the likes of the Avengers, Superman, Green Lantern and Batman.

In what should be a surprise to no one who knows him, Jayce stole the show. Everyone there knew who he was by the end of the day. He ended up wearing his Spider-Man costume with his Superman cape. He was one incredibly cute super hero, for sure.

There were people hired to be in legitimate super hero costumes—they posed with the kids and interacted with participants and onlookers alike.

Three of our friends were able to join us for the race, which we walked. Everyone dressed up and it made for a fun morning. Their presence meant a lot to us, and to me personally. Just knowing they remembered Grayden and would do something like that in his memory made for a happy and proud mommy and daddy. I continue to be in awe of the affect his death has had on the amount of people it has.

It felt good to honor him again in a manner he would've approved of. It was a good day for our family. There were bright colors everywhere and the amazing energy took control of everyone in attendance.

What made it better were the naps we all took once we got home...and the apple pie our friend Aubrey won at the raffle. Nothing seems to help a guy who just doesn't feel well like a Sunday afternoon nap and a slice of apple pie.

Jayce and Aubrey with the Lone Ranger, Superman,
Catwoman and Wonder Woman

Jamie, Kate, Erin, Jayce and I in our super hero best

Completed a 5K
with his brother

Jayce and I returned to my hometown because my sister and her family were home from Michigan for an extended weekend. Jamie was not able to come with us because of her work schedule.

It happened to be the weekend of the town celebration. There were class reunions, a parade, live music and a 5K to benefit a man I knew well and respected. He had encountered some medical issues and racked up in insane amount of medical bills in a short amount of time.

My nephew is a cross-country runner and my sister's entire family decided to run. I wanted to support the cause and thought it would be fun for Jayce so I pushed him the distance. Jayce was wearing a super hero shirt (a mini tribute to his big brother) and at the end of the course, I took him out of his stroller and he ran across the finish line to the applause of the crowd there watching. His little legs were moving as fast as I've ever seen them and there was pride in the immense smile on his face.

My nephew won the race by over a minute, but it felt like a victory to me as well. I learned there were times I had to be intentional about making new memories. Seeing Jayce's little legs motoring along accompanied by that smile is something I will never forget.

My sister and brother-in-law
had these shirts made for
their first half marathon

Gained 65 pounds (and decided enough was enough)

In November I came to an important realization, I needed to make some changes—so I went public on Facebook believing I needed the external motivation and accountability:

"I've gained 65 pounds since Grayden died...unacceptable. Going public to be embarrassed and shamed enough to do something about it. I don't have as many pictures with him as I should because I let things get out of control...before the weight gain. Lost 50 pounds with the headaches...then found 65. My clothes don't fit, I cannot breathe and I have no energy...going to do what I can to change that.

6 month challenge begins today...modest and attainable 40 pound goal to start out. Be prepared to be annoyed by weekly updates.

Game on..."

This led to three individual challenges and 20 people working together for a common goal: to achieve and live a healthier life.

Food was my medicine and I medicated a lot. The pain was real and I was searching for any semblance of relief. I didn't turn to alcohol, cigarettes or drugs, but my addiction was just as dangerous with my family's history of heart disease and stroke. I was self-destructing and it was time to stop. Silly part is, I knew this was happening for some time, but I wasn't ready to face it and take it on. I am glad that switch finally flipped.

Six weeks in, I'd lost just under 25 pounds…have a ways to go but am pleased with the progress.

Ordered pictures from our kids' photo shoots from the last two years

We are the kind of parents that have good intentions when it comes to photos and Christmas cards but often fail to complete the job.

Exhibit A: two years worth of professional pictures taken…all on discs with no printouts. We ordered pictures when Jayce was born, but it had been just under two years since our last physical order.

Do you have any idea how much kids change from the time they are a week old until they are two? Of course you do.

I do too -- and now I have the proof.

These turned out to be important because they are the last pictures we have of him alone and the final pictures we have of our entire family together.

Finalizing that memory was a necessary goal to accomplish. I can now physically see him every day… he looks exactly like the pictures in my head.

Hung pictures
in our home

I have always been a fan of living in a house that feels like a home. For me, that means I need to have pictures on the wall.

When we lost Grayden, we had two large pictures of each of the boys hanging above the fireplace and a couple of collage frames filled with Grayden's first pictures. To me, that just wasn't enough.

It was on the "to do" list for some time, but always seemed to be out-prioritized by other things—mostly my own laziness.

Once we finally ordered pictures, it was a matter of making the time to hang them. I spent a lot of time lining frames up and selecting pictures, but the results yielded a more complete sense of home.

With a notable absence in our family, the completion of our home became even more necessary. At this particular point in time, I had given up any hope that I would possess the ability to control anything. What I got back when I finally hung our pictures was a home with a complete family...and that was the reality I chose to focus on.

Talked about him regularly

We learned quickly that in many circumstances, we had become that couple: That couple who lost their son.

People didn't always know how to be around us.

We learned that is was a difficult situation for everyone involved.

People were scared to say the wrong things--so a lot of times, they said nothing at all. People were scared to talk about him—because they didn't want to say the wrong things. It was a vicious cycle.

The end result was that people were afraid to talk about him-and when we were not afraid to talk about him, it became awkward.

I was scared that people would forget about him: Forget what he meant to us and how he changed our lives. Forget his smile or his voice. Or worse yet, forget him altogether. That was the worst thing that could've happened.

I didn't talk about him to combat this, I talked about him because he was a part of my life and I was not ashamed of him or afraid to include him in my future, even if he would not be here physically to be a part of it. The fact that talking about him illustrated to others that he was not a taboo topic was merely a bonus.

I did not go out of my way to include him in my conversations. I didn't have to work hard or be intentional to include him—it was just something that was natural.

The long and short of it is this: I love my son. I am proud of my son. I miss him, but that pain is not enhanced by talking about him.

Told his brother about him

Jayce was only 15 months old when Grayden went to heaven.

He was not very verbal and I wondered for some time if he had any clue what was going on. We knew he was aware something was different—we saw him looking around corners and I know he was looking for Grayden. It was hard to watch as we really had no idea what was going on in his head.

We made it a point to talk about Grayden to Jayce as much as we could without making it unnatural. We shared stories, said his name and made sure to include phrases like "Big Brother and "best buddy."

We learned that there was no clearly defined "right way" to muddle through this. We had no choice but to make informed decisions, pray and do the best we could.

Were we worried we were making things worse? Yup.

Were we concerned we were doing more harm than good? For sure.

We had no choice but to submit to God and let him take the lead.

We would later get confirmation that Jayce was comprehending what we were saying to him. Yet another example of God's wisdom and grace.

One of our first pictures of the two of them together. He was very proud of his little brother.

This is exactly how I want to remember my boys together.

Told my wife I wanted to have another baby

When we had Jayce, Jamie was content for our family to be complete at four. I had always wanted a bigger family but Jamie's pregnancies and post-pregnancies were not easy and I understood her desire to only have two children.

Even though I understood, I was still holding out hope that we might be able to have another. After all, I wanted a shot to have a little girl—and would've been fine had we had another boy. After all, we were already proficient in raising boys.

I think that because I was never really content being "done" at two, the idea of having another was not a big deal to me. And likewise, because Jamie believed we were done, the idea of having another child somehow seemed to lend itself to the idea that a new baby would conceivably be viewed as a replacement to Grayden.

The very first picture of the three most important people in my life together.

When I told Jamie I wanted to have another baby, her response was one of uncertainty—and I completely understood where she was coming from.

With a little help from our grief counselor, we realized our struggles with this particular issue (that a baby might be viewed as a replacement for Grayden) was just fear taking over.

So much of our lives had become about fear: The fear that we will feel this way forever. The fear that something else will happen that we cannot recover from. The fear that the same thing will happen to Jayce.

Fear effected the way we thought, the way we made decisions, the way saw everything really.

Once we were asked the question, "why wouldn't we have a baby?" and had nothing of substance in response, we realized that our hesitancy to take that chance was a result of fear.

We knew how fear could be paralyzing. We understood how fear had changed us and in this instance, we were able to say, "enough is enough." This was a small step to regain our identity.

It was a change of mindset and a leap of faith.

We would be scared of a lot of things, the perception of other people on this matter would not be one of them.

We were open to our family expanding, and it had nothing to do with Grayden. When he was with us, we took pride in living life with no regrets—this is a fine example of our family doing things the way we want to do them: With an eye on our future and without regret. God willing, we will soon be a family of five.

Ordered a primary colors windmill sculpture

On a family vacation with Jamie's family, we spent the better part of a week in a relatively close "touristy" town. It was a short drive for us and we got a giant condo-like place with separate rooms. We spent some time on the river and had a good time.

While we were there, we walked along the main street and went into some little shops. One of the places we ended up was a metal sculpture shop. Their displays were awesome—and they had a little bit of everything. Immediately, we were drawn to a brightly colored double windmill. Painted with red, blue, yellow and green, it really read little boy. In talking, Jamie and I realized we both wanted one for Grayden's playground. We had decided to ask about the price because we liked it so much that we were considering one for the memorial garden in the front of our house as well.

The lady we spoke to was the primary artist-she was sculptor, welder and artist all in one…and an extremely nice woman, as well. After a short conversation with her, we found out the double windmill sold for $400. They were worth every penny, but realistically speaking, were a bit too expensive for us to purchase two. So instead of moving forward with the idea to purchase one for the playground at church and one for our memorial garden at home, we decided to purchase one to be placed at the site of the playground.

Jamie noticed a small display for a local organization called "Angel Wings." There was a sign posted that all the proceeds for a particular item in the store go directly to benefit this particular organization.

We asked the lady if she could give us more information and she told us it was an organization that raised money for children (and their families) with debilitating illnesses and injuries.

Having recently lost Grayden, we were attracted to the idea of supporting this cause.

We shared with her our desire to support such an organization citing our recent story and I was humbled by her response. Immediately, she asked us if she could give us a hug and apologized for what we had been enduring. Then she went on to ask about the specifics. We shared his story and told her about him.

From there, we told her we'd inquired about the primary colors-based windmill sculpture because wanted to place it at our church on site at his memorial playground.

It flies every day…
and I think of him.

I noticed the lady gathering her thoughts and she eloquently said to us, "Would you allow me to donate one to the playground in his honor?" Jamie and I looked at each other and shared duplicate tears as I responded, "you would do that for him?" Her response, was simple, "It would be an honor if you would let me."

At this point, our tears had become more prominent and we told her what a special gift she was giving us. It was a priceless moment…but it wasn't over yet.

Knowing we'd already decided to purchase one, and were interested in another, I thanked her again and told her we would like to place an order for an additional sculpture to be placed at our memorial garden at our home. Without blinking, she responded by saying, "Well, why don't I just donate two?"

Humbled and taken aback, I mumbled something to the effect of "oh no ma'am, you don't need to do that, we are glad to purchase one"

She quickly responded saying, "Please let me do this, I would love to be able to do this for your family."

At this point, I was emotionally spent. I hugged the woman yet again and thanked her profusely as I tried to speak clearly through the mess of tears and blubbering I was encountering.

Her response, "It really is my pleasure…God bless you"

He did…at that moment.

God blessed us through the actions of this lady, my new favorite artist. Her generosity and simple act, changed me that day—and that is not me being over-emotional or attention seeking.

This was the first time we'd encountered something like this and its impact was powerful.

I will never forget this woman and her amazing gift to our family and community. It will be illustrated every time the piece spins. It will be fluid and graceful. It will be bright and happy. It will represent energy and movement—all things I am reminded of when I think of my boy.

Went to a ton of Cardinals games

We love Cardinals baseball at our house. Plain and simple.

Because we live in St. Louis, we have been able to go to a lot of games. There are always tickets available, and when we find them for the right price (which for us means really, really cheap) we take advantage every chance we get.

Jamie used to work at a large church and because her office space was by the main entrance, when people would come in with their tickets that they could not use, she often had the first chance to scoop them up. As these were generally fantastic seats, we loved these instances.

As Jamie is no longer working there, our free ticket opportunities have dwindled. Craigslist and StubHub have been good outlets (I once got tickets on two consecutive days for less than $2 a ticket…weekday series against subpar teams are good for that)

Jayce and I rooting on the Redbirds at a home game.

Because people know we are big Redbird fans, we had a lot of opportunities to attend games this season. Our friends were looking for ways to help us, to pick us up, and ballgames were a good way to spend time with them and do something we sincerely enjoy all at the same time.

I went to 14 games that season, including game five of the World Series. The Cardinals were 12-2 when I was there. I think I should go to every game as my winning percentage is pretty darned good. Our only losses were a Saturday evening game (to the rotten, stinking Cubs) and Game 5 of the World Series—I wish we had those back.

Our family and friends continued to find ways to spend time with us, take our minds off our horrid reality and let us know we were in their thoughts.

As we learned how to grieve, we noticed one thing: Someone was always there—and I cannot tell you how grateful I am for that.

I know it was not always easy for everyone to want to be around us. We presented a difficult and awkward situation a lot of times. That has nothing to do with us, it is just a natural and logical response to our situation. Our pain was unknown and uncomfortable…and when our friends and family pushed through that and were there every time we turned around, we noticed.

Hooked up a family at Christmas

Last Christmas, our neighbor Scott randomly showed up with numerous gifts for our family. He told us he knew we'd encountered some unfortunate luck and that he wanted to be a part of making our Christmas a little bit brighter.

Jamie and I, having fallen on some hard times financially because I had to forfeit my job due to the migraines, had decided we would not exchange Christmas gifts and that we would only fill a stocking for the boys.

This killed us, but we knew it was the correct decision. Grayden was only two and a half and Jayce was just 14 months old. They would not remember and would certainly not go without as the rest of our family would pick up our slack. Our boys were loved and even though it hurt our pride, eliminating Christmas gifts was the right thing to do.

As this would be Grayden's last Christmas with us, I cannot tell you what Scott's gift meant to us. Grayden was excited. He played with those toys until the day he went to be with Jesus. It brought him so much joy…and provided his parents with the lasting memory of watching him open Christmas presents in his home one final time.

Because of what this meant to our family, Jamie and I have since decided we will do this for another family every year.

We were fortunate enough to pitch this idea to a group of our friends and they were completely on board to be a part of this as well.

Every year, my buddies from college get together two times: once the first weekend in December for our annual gigging trip, and the second, the weekend after the 4th of July for the AB Golf Classic.

We pirated the group idea from the latter.

Each year, the hosting couple purchases dinner on Friday night and asks everyone who eats to donate what they would've spent on dinner for some identified charitable donation. This year, the money went for the memorial playground we are building for Grayden at our church.

Obviously, that meant a lot to us and was even more of a motivation to give back.

So when we held our first annual Christmas board game decathlon party with a group of our friends, Jamie and I decided to provide the food and ask for a donation to be used to provide gifts to a family at Christmas.

Everyone was on board, and we have adopted it as something that will happen every time we get together.

The family we selected was a single mother with five children. We were able to provide them with 65 gifts. A truly awesome experience and one I cannot wait to recreate with another family next year.

It might look like a normal Christmas tree,
but to one family, it meant a lot more than that.

Waited for autopsy results

After five months, Grayden's autopsy had been finalized and his cause of death was ruled as "complications from a seizure disorder."

Being a bit concerned as we were repeatedly told by our doctors he did not have a seizure disorder, I called my brother-in-law, who is a forensic pathologist to see if they were somehow able to diagnose a seizure disorder through the autopsy. He let us know that they were not able to find anything else and that this was a more generic term utilized because he had a history of seizures. Had he never had a seizure, the C.O.D. would have been "undetermined."

For five months they sent out more slides trying to find something to attribute this to...but it seems as though our initial thoughts have been confirmed, Grayden's death was a horrid fluke.

Strangely, this was good news. I find comfort in the fact that we did not miss anything and that our original thoughts have been confirmed.

We miss him every day and he is still, and will always be, a part of our lives. It is our hope that now, with this information, we can feel something that might resemble closure and we can move on.

Watched hundreds of balloons be released and seemingly disappear

After Grayden's funeral, we decided to have a balloon release in his honor. Our friends arranged for this to happen and balloons were given to those in attendance.

Prior to the release, I stood in the middle of our family and friends and said, "These are for our boy."

As I let mine go, so did everyone else. The mass of balloons lifted towards heaven and everyone was silent as we watched them elevate.

It was a surreal silence and then, as if God had opened a magic door letting them in, the balloons were gone.

The balloon release following the funeral

Painted a super hero bedroom

Every time we walked into his room, we were reminded of him. It was comforting and heart-breaking simultaneously.

The room, the way it was, was what he knew. The only issue was, that he was no longer with us and it was no longer this room.

Shortly after we lost him, we made the decision to move Jayce into that room. It was the right thing.

However, the existing room, was not Jayce's room…and he deserved to have his own room.

After talking with Jamie, we decided on a Super Hero theme. We'd hoped we would still feel Grayden in there while giving Jayce a space of his own…with his own identity represented in it.

It was simple, but with deep meaning—it was what I'd hoped for.

I converted the existing yellow room, complete with animal faces from Grayden's first bedding set and a giant jungle mural (both painted all over the walls,) into a primary color, super hero infested room that Jayce loved.

The new bedroom. My favorite part was watching
Jayce repeatedly ask visitors if he could show them his room.

Re-surfaced
my deck

It might seem trivial and odd to highlight this, but completing this particular task was the first tangible thing I felt like I accomplished since we lost him.

For so long, we were in *survive* mode—and that doesn't work for me.

If I am going to be successful I need to be in *thrive* mode. For too long, I had let the hurt consume and control me.

Resurfacing our deck was a big job as far as the amount of time it would take me to complete it…but one that was attainable. It would not be difficult, it would just be time consuming. This was a problem because at this point, time was the enemy.

When I committed to completing it, in a strange way, I took back a little control. It was a minor victory, but a victory nonetheless.

At that time in my life, a victory—even a small one, was worth noting.

Mourned with our Bible study

We met weekly with our Bible study. They were our friends and, in many cases, our extended family.

Grayden's death touched many people. The makeup of our group…17 adults and 14 kids, made it a bit more real. I am still humbled by the love they showed him…and us.

It was such a blessing to watch them comfort and care for us, for each other and our children.

We had meals set up every other day. Someone was assigned to come to our house once a week to help us with groceries and another day weekly to help with basic household chores and cleaning.

We were not alone, even though sometimes we felt like it.

They respected our privacy but were an appropriate, positive presence. They asked us questions and listened to our answers.

One of my favorites stories is also one of the most heartbreaking.

Evie, the three and a half year old daughter of our good friends, was processing what was happening. He mother told us she seemed puzzled and a bit sad in saying, "Do you mean he won't be able to grow up with us?"

Hearing those words broke my heart. Hearing what she said next restored it… and I was reminded how smart kids really are.

"But that's okay mommy, because he is in heaven and Jesus loves him."

Went to a World Series game

Jayce's birthday happened to fall on a Friday this particular year. Jamie was able to take the day off and we went to a pumpkin patch.

The pumpkin patch was pretty cool. Complete with a hayrack ride, kiddie tractors, hay tunnels and various other rides, Jayce (and mommy and daddy) had a ball.

We went back home around naptime to recharge for the rest of the evening.

Jayce was in bed, I was reclined in the chair and Jamie went to the bathroom. I was half asleep when she came around the corner and asked me what we had planned for Monday evening.

My initial response was one of mild annoyance—she just walked by the calendar in the hall where our "social calendar" is…why didn't she just look?

The next thing she said legitimately took my breathe away:

"Well, if we don't have anything else going on, then we can go to the World Series game because I just won tickets through work!"

I asked how she found out and she told me she got a text from a friend of hers at work. After a brief instance in which I threatened to burn her house down if she was joking, Jamie confirmed that she did, in fact, win two tickets to game five of the 2013 World Series.

Enter my anxiety…I suggested Jamie go pick up the tickets. She agreed but wasn't walking out the door. So again, I suggested she go pick up the tickets… but she was not walking out the door.

Finally, I had to break it down for her.

"Honey, I think you need to get in the car and go pick up those tickets immediately…like right now. I do not want to risk them be given way to someone else because we didn't get there in time to pick them up."

Recognizing the urgency in my voice, Jamie gave in to my pushiness and completely irrational lack of comfort and left immediately to pick up the tickets.

When she returned, she was holding two tickets in section 136. My heart was beating fast and I would be able to cross a bucket list item off.

In the end, the wrong team won but we had a great time and experienced something we will likely never experience again.

While I was sad to experience this without him, I was thrilled to share this moment with Jamie.

I was reminded of Grayden's first trip to the ballpark. The Cubs were in town and it was an afternoon game during the week. Because I was working in student activities at the time, the Cardinals sent an offer for extremely discounted tickets. This never happens for Cards-Cubs games so it was something that took me little time to take advantage of.

Jamie and I took both boys--and what made the day better was that all of our parents were able to attend.

We had our day at the ballpark…it wasn't a World Series game but I would trade it for nothing.

Got a personalized
Bears jersey

GSH doesn't really stand for Grayden Steele Hickenbottom.

A package came in the mail that Jamie told me I could not open. I had no clue what it was, but as often happens with such a mystery package, I was intrigued and excited as I was pretty sure in some capacity, it would benefit me.

Jamie came down the stairs at her sister's house (we were hanging out with them for the evening and got there before they got home) wearing a Chicago Bears Jersey. As I am a die-hard Bears fan, I was excited.

The number on the jersey was 25. I was perplexed how she would know I wanted a Matt Suhey jersey. He was the fullback on the '85 that wore #25. (I would later find out he wore #26)

When she turned around, I found out the jersey said "GRAYDEN" on the back. It was so cool.

Jamie told me she'd been wanting to do something fun for me for some time and when she recognized the initials "GSH" on the sleeve of the jersey, she knew she was on to something.

She called her Aunt Denise, who is a big Bears fan herself, and lives much closer to Chicago. Jamie was afraid she'd run into issues trying to find anything other than a Rams jersey here in St. Louis.

After a bit of research, they made the order. The jersey ended up being a gift from Aunt Denise via Jamie's idea. It was yet another example of people lifting us up with fantastic memorials for our boy.

They selected the number 25 because Grayden was 2.5 years old when he went to be with Jesus. I took every opportunity I had to explain to people that Grayden shared initials with the great George S. Halas.

I wore the jersey every chance I got--even to Cardinals games. It was an instant source of pride and regular part of my wardrobe. A living memorial that made allowed me to be a proud daddy. It was perfect.

Sang at a wedding he was supposed to be in

Grayden had captured a part of many people's hearts. "Aunt Whitney" was no exception.

Whitney was one of my former students. But she was not an ordinary student. I have a group of 25-30 students I still keep in contact with on a regular basis.

Whitney is one of about 5 or 6 that regularly come to visit our family. She is a mainstay in our house and our boys know her as "Aunt Whitney." When she got engaged to Tony, they asked if Grayden would be their ring bearer--We were so excited.

The day he died, Jamie recognizing Grayden would not be able to be in their wedding is one of the clearest memories I have. We were talking in our living room, surrounded by family and friends and in the middle of a sentence, Jamie stopped, said, "He's not going to be able to be in Tony and Whitney's wedding." And then she cried...we both did.

It was the first clear thought we had about something he would miss. It would be the first of many painful realities.

They got married a couple months after we lost him. It was a great day. Fantastic energy, great people and a really good time.

They'd asked me to sing at the ceremony. It was my 95th wedding so nerves were not an issue for me. I always enjoy being a part of weddings so even if it wasn't Whitney and Tony's, I would've been excited. The fact that it was, elevated my level of commitment and served as motivation to perform well.

Despite battling a bit of a bug, I was pleased with the music we made. I got to sing with one of my best friend's, Jason, and I am confident we added to their special day.

My only issue was watching the ring bearer walk down the aisle. It was bittersweet, but luckily I was in the middle of a verse and didn't have the chance to react.

We had little baseball-like cards made and Whitney put one under the unity candle. It was only a symbolic presence, but I loved that the day was not completely void of him.

After the ceremony, we got to enjoy the atmosphere. We saw a ton of former students and had a great evening.

Whitney's parents thanked me for being a part of the day, citing they felt many people would've opted out. Not going was never an option. We hated that he wasn't there with us, but letting our pain control our decision making would've tarnished his memory…and we would never be okay with that.

Jayce, Tony, Whitney, Jamie and I celebrating their day. Grayden was supposed to be a ring bearer but instead got to watch from heaven.

Kissed him for the final time

At the front of our church, in a room full of our family and friends, I leaned over his casket, kissed him on the lips and then the forehead one last time and said, "Go be with God, my boy…mommy and daddy will be there soon. I love you"

Wore a Superman shirt and a cape to his funeral

After mulling our options, Jamie and I decided on matching Superman shirts for the funeral. Out friend Erin made our entire bible study "G" buttons and everyone wore them. The capes were a gift from my students—what an addition they were.

My outfit was completed with a Captain America band-aid on the side of my head. (I cut it shaving and couldn't get it to stop bleeding.)

It was not traditional funeral attire…but this was not a regular funeral—we made sure of that.

Dave, Jen and I celebrating my boy.

Counted over 5,000 Facebook likes, messages and comments in less than a week

For the first week after he died, I spent a lot of time on Facebook. I read the things people wrote…and when I had read everything, I started over and read them again.

There is something about the massive amount of support we received that helped me to realize that we were going to be "okay."

My dad asked me if I had counted the number of responses we'd received. And to that point, I had not—I literally had no idea how many messages and responses we'd received…I just knew it was a lot.

One night at about two in the morning when I was struggling to sleep, I began to count. Long story short, in 6 days, I stopped counting when I reached 5,000.

His death was a real thing to a ton of different people. Whether people had experienced it or not, they recognized the magnitude of what had happened. And although they could not understand directly, they could imagine.

Drove away without him for the first time

The first road trip we made without him was an emotional one. At different times, my wife and I both had emotional responses to the idea that we were travelling without him.

Over the course of our three hour trip, we had our moments. Once we arrived at my parents' house, things seemed to settle down—until it was time to leave.

We said our goodbyes and I struggled. I am not one to fight tears so I did not. I cried, and it was a necessary release. Getting through goodbyes was only the beginning.

As we backed out of the driveway, I had to stop the car.

It was wrong that he was not with us. My wife asked me if we needed to go back but I knew that would solve nothing.

This would be part of our new reality. When we went, he would not go with us. When we returned, we would return without him.

I hated it, but me hating it would not eliminate it from being so.

So we did what made sense. We drove home--and we were alright.

Gave his Christmas pajamas to a friend

So Jamie and I are frugal…or just cheap.

To save money, and to make a dollar go a bit further, we shop the after holiday sales when things are on clearance. Fifty and seventy-five percent off are some of my favorite prices.

Each year at Christmas, we decided to do family pajamas as one of our Christmas traditions. In the spirit of being frugal, it made sense to look for pajamas after the season, right?

We found some pretty sweet reindeer PJ's for the boys at seventy percent off and bought them in the sizes we anticipated the boys would be in the following year.

The day after he died, I went to our gift closet to look for something and found his Christmas pajamas. We had bought them just a few weeks prior.

I had a pretty strong emotional response to seeing them and I just held them for a while. They still had the tags on them so returning them would've been an option, but I couldn't make myself do that.

Those were his…they were bought for him.

I just didn't like the idea of some stranger wearing his pajamas.

I asked Jamie if it would be okay if we gave them to one of our friend's kids and she seemed to like the idea.

Our friends Barry and Christa came over and their son Evan was having a ball in the backyard. He was playing like Grayden did. He used his manners like Grayden did. He seemed to really love life like Grayden did.

He was the one--Jamie and I agreed.

I asked Barry if he could come upstairs and we had a conversation about the pajamas. Barry said it would be an honor for Evan to wear them but he asked me to give them to him.

Grayden in his
Christmas jammies

Barry called for Evan to come upstairs and he came up immediately. When he walked in the room, Barry bent down so he would be on his level then following conversation played out:

"Ev, Brent has something very special to ask you. Do you remember Grayden…the little boy we have been talking about?"

"Yes"

"And do you remember what we talked about?"

"Yeah, he was a boy like me but he died…and lots of people are sad."

"That's right…and where is Grayden now?"

"He's in Heaven."

"That's right, Ev."

I wept at this. This is the exact conversation I would imagine I would've had with Grayden if situations had been different.

Evan asked me if I was Grayden's daddy and I told him I was. He asked me if I was sad and I told him I was.

His innocence was powerful and was exactly what I needed at that precise moment.

I showed Evan the pajamas and asked him if he would like to have them. I told him we'd already bought them and that because he would not be able to wear them that we needed someone else to.

He was so excited and wanted to try them on immediately.

I saw so much of Grayden in him. It was comforting and refreshing. I allowed myself to enjoy it but after that moment, I made a conscious decision to stop drawing comparisons. Evan didn't deserve that kind of pressure from anyone. To be honest, it was probably pressure that he would never feel, but I knew whether he realized it or not, that it wasn't fair to him.

I remember that moment well.

We made the right decision.

Shared his stuffed animals with a cousin

Jayce and I had started a weekly playdate with my cousin's little girls. On a week when they came to our house, Sophie (who was just a bit younger than Grayden) was playing with toys.

She brought out a stuffed Panda bear and said, "Mommy, look, a panda."

My cousin acknowledged her by saying, "Ooh Sophie, you love pandas, don't you? That is so cool."

I told Sophie that she was playing with her cousin Grayden's panda bear and asked her if she would like to take it home with her.

My cousin looked at me and nodded her head as if to say, "we do not need to take Grayden's panda bear home with us."

So I responded by saying, we have two of those (each of our boys had one) and I would love it if you would take it home and play with it every day.

My cousin, realizing it really would mean a lot to me if they would take the bear, asked Sophie to thank me and smiled a bittersweet smile as she agreed.

She talked to Sophie about how special this bear was and Sophie just hugged the bear tightly.

The bear had a new home...and even if she never re-told it, Sophie had her very own Grayden story—I loved that.

Went ice skating with his mom and laughed for the first time since we lost him

Jamie and I in Michigan at our marriage conference

Jamie and I decided early on in our marriage that we would attend a marriage seminar every year.

Five years into our marriage, we'd yet to make one.

After a little research, Jamie found one in Michigan about an hour from my sister's house and we'd made plans for them to watch the boys while we went to the seminar. It was a perfect "kill two birds with one stone" sort of thing.

Then Grayden didn't wake up from his nap one Monday afternoon.

Having made plans to attend this weekend retreat only a couple weeks after his funeral, we decided it would be good for us all to go ahead and make it happen.

At this seminar, we had assignments and mandatory date nights. I did some investigating and found an ice skating rink within walking distance of our hotel…and we made a quick appearance there prior to our dinner at a dueling piano bar.

We got our skates laced up and made our way to the rink. Our ankles weak and our skating experience nearly non-existent, we set out to not break any bones… and then we laughed. We only went around three times, and that was enough.

It was innocent, without sadness and perfect.

I am sure we laughed sometime in that month and a half, but this was the first time we recognized it and felt no guilt.

As more time passed, it became easier to laugh.

I, for one, am most thankful for this. Life is so much easier to live when laughter can be present.

Put a memorial sticker on my vehicle

The first of two stickers came from our friends Roger and Shelley. They had them printed and I was thrilled to get it.

When I finally was able to put it on our van, it looked great. Occasionally, someone will ask about it—and I love that because it gives me a chance to tell them about him.

And once we had ours, our friends and family wanted them, too. Jamie had a friend from high school that now runs a printing business and she contacted him to see if he would be able and interested in creating about 50 stickers for us.

We shared our ideas and he sent back some specs for us to choose from. The designs were brilliant and we ordered 50.

When we tried to arrange for payment, he informed us that he would take care of any cost. His amazing gift contributed to Grayden's legacy in a manner that we will never understand.

Every time a person sees one, there is an opportunity that his story can be told.

Failed to sleep at night

I couldn't sleep…and when I did, it was not for long. I was awake for three days after he died and the more I tried to sleep, the more difficult it became.

I couldn't help replaying everything that had happened. Finding him haunted me. I was worried I would see that same picture every time I closed my eyes.

To be honest, I think I was setting myself up for disaster.

I was sad, scared and completely disconnected from reality. I spent my days surrounding myself with family and friends. I hugged and kissed hundreds of people. I cried with most of them.

When I should've been sleeping, I found several other things to pass the time. I read. I looked at pictures. I cried. I vomited. I battled headaches. I watched videos of him.

I was overwhelmed, miserable and reeling.

In time, I figured out a way to sleep. It was the first of many battles I would face.

Remembered him

This happened every day, multiple times a day.

There are times when I worry about forgetting some of the little things…and that breaks my heart. But I never worry about forgetting him—how could I?

I remember him by telling his story. I remember him by watching videos and looking at pictures. I remember him every time I close my eyes.

I honor him by working to become a better father to his brother and a better husband to his mother. I still want to be something he can be proud of.

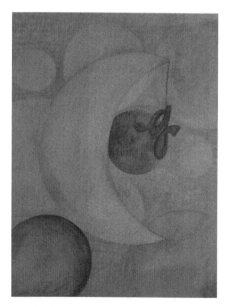

Another painting...his death reminded me how much I like to create--and I used that outlet as a source of healing

Bought new furniture
for our living room

Shortly after he died, we saw him everywhere, and it was painful.

Our home was his home, and that did not cease just because he was no longer here with us.

When we looked in the living room, I saw the couch he jumped off of. When I went in the bathroom, I saw the exact place he stood when he unrolled all of the toilet paper. When I looked out the kitchen window, I saw the swing he spent the majority of his time in when we first took him outside regularly.

And when we saw these things, what we felt was sadness and pain.

In an effort to eliminate some of this from happening, and not because we were running from anything, we decided to start looking into some different living room furniture to switch things up a bit. We had been given a gift that was to be used to "pick ourselves up" when we needed it and this seemed to be the perfect way to make a necessary change and improve our surroundings at the same time.

We started by looking at new furniture and quickly realized that that was not in the cards for us. Financially, we just could not make that happen.

So we turned to Craigslist. Jamie is a bit of a germaphobe and was against the idea of purchasing used furniture. However, she agreed that if we could find a good, used leather set that it could be sanitized and she would be comfortable with it in our home.

Luckily for us, we found a set that looked great and was in our price range. When I made the call, we were the first in line and the lady I was speaking with seemed eager to complete the transaction. In speaking with her, we made plans to meet up and I made the drive to her house.

When I got there, she showed me an extremely nice living room set that was of very high quality. She had the original sales receipts and it was a high priced set that seemed to be of high quality.

She went on to say that she didn't really want to get rid of it, but had run into some hard times after being laid off and needed the money to pay rent. She went on to say that her husband left her when she was pregnant with twins and that she had accepted custody of her sister's daughter because she was unable to care for her herself. The long and short of it was, she was now raising four children by herself and did not have a steady income.

In talking with her and her boyfriend, I shared with them the reason we were looking for new furniture, citing we needed to freshen things up and make a change. I learned that he'd lost his son nearly ten years ago and I immediately felt an enhanced connection to them.

I did not like the idea of her family not having living room furniture so I asked her if she would consider accepting our current set. Our plan was to try to move it to our basement where we hold our bible study, but we were unsure it would fit. When this opportunity presented itself, I felt like I should present it as an option.

With tears in the corner of her eyes, she graciously accepted our offer and thanked me. I loved how it completed an amazing story.

Later that evening she sent me a picture message with all four kids on the couch. It was accompanied with a message that read – "It fits perfectly—thank you so much for doing this for our family."

Cried with my brother

Kurt and I in our sister's wedding years ago—he's a lot older than me!

My brother, Kurt, is a successful basketball coach and January is state tournament time for Illinois Junior High Boys basketball.

His seventh grade team was undefeated heading into the postseason. Ironically, two of my cousin's kids played on that team.

When Grayden died, I called Kurt and told him to stick around for practice and come down when he could get here. His team was playing in the state quarterfinals the night before the funeral and they needed their coach. I come from a family of coaches and have coached myself so I get this…plus, there was nothing he could do but drive to St. Louis and be sad with us. What we needed was for him to prep his squad and get a victory…and that is what he did.

Kurt rode down the morning of the funeral with my cousins, Eric and Steph. I saw him come in the back of the church about 45 minutes before services were supposed to begin. I walked back to greet him and I could see that he was visibly shaken but trying to maintain his composure. He gave me a hug and I asked him if he wanted to go see Grayden…after a brief pause, he said, "yeah."

Kurt grabbed my hand and we walked down the aisle at the church to where my boy lay—peaceful and serene.

Kurt looked at him, shook his head as if he was trying to talk himself into believing what he was seeing was really okay, all the time trying not to cry—but seeing his nephew in that state was too much for him…and it would've been for anyone.

Kurt grabbed me and hugged me harder than he ever had before and we sobbed, unable to speak.

It was a welcomed moment for me as Kurt and I hadn't always been as close as I wanted us to be. It was great and horrible all at the same time--I hated it and loved it simultaneously.

Grayden's gift to us at that particular time was *that* moment. I know he was smiling as he looked down on us and I am thankful that my little boy was able to bring people together…I just hate that the cost was his death.

Thought bad things about kids who were not well-behaved... and then vowed not to be 'that person'

I struggled with this a lot initially.

I would see kids acting out and be frustrated because they were still here and Grayden was not.

I found myself thinking the following:

- "Grayden would never have acted like that."

- "They will never be a beneficial part of society. Why are they here and my boy isn't?"

- "They don't have a chance."

That is the gist of what was going on in my extremely hurt and extremely judgmental head. I was angry at his loss. I was angry at the loss of his potential here on earth.

My anger led to statements I do not know to be true.

Did I feel guilty? Yes.

Did I have a problem with the way my mind was working? Yes.

Did this keep on going for long? No.

I decided that person was not who I wanted to be. I made the change and was (luckily) successful in doing so.

My bitterness faded and my heart began the restoration process.

Went to his grave
for the first time

The cemetery is a place we were not prepared for. At least not to go visit Grayden there. And to complicate things, we don't believe that is where he is. I know there is something to be said about his final resting place, but when I go to cemeteries, I don't go there to "see" people. I go there because of the illustration of earthly connection it provides.

Nonetheless, there is that connection.

We talked about what it means to not always feel like we need to go to the cemetery because we do not believe he is there…and we are okay with that. I don't need to see a grave marker to possess the ability to talk to him.

We have decided we will not feel obligated to go on his birthday, the anniversary of his death, mother's day or father's day…instead, we decided we would go when we felt like it.

On a random day, Jamie and I took Jayce to the cemetery. As we made the walk to his plot, it was hard to breathe. We told Jayce about this special place and told him about his big brother.

Jamie had a more difficult outward reaction than I did this particular time and even though I probably appeared to be numb, I was not. I held my son and my wife as we collectively missed a part of our family.

Jamie took Jayce and returned to the car because it was cold…and I just stood there. I don't remember what I was thinking or feeling…but I do remember just being there.

Wished I could dream about him

I wanted to see him…and I convinced myself that dreaming about him would be a way to feed that desire.

Every time I closed my eyes I saw his face, but it wasn't as vivid as I wanted it to be. It wasn't real and I hungered for that.

Maybe I thought I would be able to talk to him or play with him or pick him up and kiss him again. Maybe I hoped it would feel like he was here again. Maybe I just wanted to believe it could happen.

Maybe… maybe I put my hopes in the wrong place.

The day after he died, our babysitter told us she had a dream about him. It was soothing and calming to her…and provided me with a sense of hope.

Miss Hannah with our boys…she helped raise them

In her dream, Grayden told her he loved her. He said not to worry because Jesus loves him. He let her know that in heaven, you don't have to take naps… and then he told her it will all be okay.

My immediate response was of pride. I remember thinking that Grayden was advanced… even in heaven—God sent him out on assignment on his first day.

The truth is, Hannah needed to have that dream…and at the time I was envious. I wanted it to be me.

In the first year after we lost him, I didn't dream about him a single time.

But it hasn't mattered.

Once the initial shock of losing him faded, I was able to clearly see him every time I closed my eyes.

I no longer felt the desire to dream about him to feel connected to him. And I realized that anything I had hoped to say to him in a dream I could still say to him at any point throughout the day.

Started dressing his little brother in his clothes

When we lost Grayden, Jayce was 15 months old. At the time, Jayce wore Grayden's clothes and we would occasionally find ourselves saying things like, "Oh, I remember when Grayden wore that. Wasn't that what he wore that one time when" such and such happened?

Of course we had our favorites, (some of which had been passed down from my sister's kids) but really taking notice of this didn't become prominent until after he died.

We faced physical memories.

And even though there body shapes were completely different and they didn't wear the clothes the same way, there were definite moments when Jayce looked more like Grayden when he was wearing his clothes.

The high-energy shirt is my mom's favorite.

Every time Jayce wears the light green, long sleeved high energy shirt, I am transformed to Grayden standing at the top of the slide sporting his giant dimples.

I used to wonder if that was a gift or a curse.

I used to believe that whether it was a gift or a curse depended on the day, on the moment or on the current attitude we possessed...but I was wrong.

I really believe that is dependent solely upon us. If we choose to make it a moment of sadness, then sadness will take over. However, if we choose to see the similarities in our boys, we draw connection to them and, in the process, cultivate the love we have for each of them.

I love the memories we have of Grayden in clothes Jayce now wears. I look forward to Jayce providing us with many similar memories to hold on to.

Put his train in a Rubbermaid tote

Our friends asked us if we wanted them to come around. They were being considerate to the idea that having children around might be painful for us.

Our response was simple: We want to be surrounded by our family and friends. And yes, bring your kids. We want to feed off their energy and enjoy their innocence. We want our house to be filled with noise. We want them to play with his toys, to break his toys like he would've. It is a normal part of growing up—and we hungered for normal. We let them know that if there were special toys to us, that we would take it upon ourselves to make them unavailable… and we did just that.

We put Grayden's wooden train set upstairs in a clear tote. It will stay there until the day when we introduce it to Jayce. We will tell him about the train and talk to him about his brother—this will not be something he is unaccustomed to.

This will probably happen before too much longer. My wife hates it when I use "before too long" as a point of reference. I guess in this case, only Jamie and I will know when that is.

My niece took this picture… what you cannot see is his five cousins surrounding him. They were never too far from him.

Experienced his third birthday without him

And it sucked.

He killed a cupcake when he turned one and we watched and laughed.

He partied at the pool when he was two and we took note as we swam with him.

On his third birthday, he was in the arms of Jesus watching *us* live our lives as we missed him.

Grayden on his first and second birthdays

Bought my wife a moonstone ring

Jamie and Grayden were both born in June. Generally, it seems as amethyst and pearl are the gemstones most associated with June.

When I did a little digging, (and my wife brought it to my attention) I discovered that moonstone was actually an identified June birthstone as well. In conjunction with the message from Grayden's funeral, it became important to me that I get Jamie some sort of moonstone jewelry.

I thought about a bracelet, pendant or necklace but could not find the right piece. I figured a ring was probably the way to go as Jamie wears rings daily and does a good job of rotating different rings in and out of the rotation.

I found what I thought was the perfect choice rather quickly.

To be sure, I looked for about three more days before making the purchase. Finding nothing that spoke to me more, I bought the ring and waited anxiously to give it to her.

It was a ring already in her size (a sign, I convinced myself) with three round moonstones, which I believed could represent Jamie, Jayce and I as we mourned the loss of our little super hero…our son and brother.

The moonstones were a representation of Grayden, their round shape an illustration of God's love for us, even when it is difficult for us to recognize.

Even though I thought it was perfect, Jamie and I have severely different taste. I wanted her to love this, not because of what it stood for in my mind, but because she genuinely thought it was pretty.

She is a pretty easy read for me, and I can say with some certainty that she didn't hate it.

Do I count that as victory?

Only if she thinks of our family every time she puts it on.

Missed him most at night

I feared the quiet, so it should not have surprised me that the evenings would be difficult for me.

When Jamie and Jayce were asleep, the silence was deafening and paralyzing.

You see, when I have downtime, I generally spend it thinking and analyzing. At this particular time in my life, those things were not a good combination for me.

Unfortunately, that is how I spent most of my evenings for the months after.

When it was quiet, I missed him the most. When I missed him most, I felt the most lonely. When I felt the most lonely, the quiet became more intense...

It was a horrid cycle and I was stuck in the middle of it.

They say time heals all wounds--I disagree.

I struggle to believe anything can heal this. The only thing that makes this better is him being back here—and we all know that cannot happen.

I do believe that it will get better, and the last year has proven that.

Every day you make an effort, you learn how to handle things a bit better. Every day you fight the silence, the anxiety lessens in intensity. Every day you face the sadness, you breathe a bit easier. Most importantly of all, every day you carry on, you are one day closer to seeing him or her again.

Thanked God for the time we had with him

Here's what it came down to…

I wanted him back with us…but he wasn't coming back.

I was facing two potential options as I moved forward.

One-- I could curse God, turn my back and run the other direction (and forfeit my chance to experience heaven in the process.)

Or…

Two-- I could embrace God, even though I didn't understand his purpose in taking Grayden (and lean on the only source of comfort I could identify with in the process)

Shortly after, I didn't want to want or need God. But the truth is, I could only find comfort in Him. You can imagine how confusing that was, right? The only thing that works is something I don't want, because that thing (at least theoretically) caused me to experience pain, sadness and discomfort.

Ultimately, my decision was an easy one. You see, I like to debate—it is how I learn. I like challenge—to challenge and be challenged (not attacked). My struggle with this was that I could not come up with any possible scenario in which I won a debate with God. And even if I did, I still didn't have my boy with me. I would still miss him growing up, learning to drive and going off to college.

So I came to the decision that blaming God and letting my life become about bitterness and pain was a waste of my life…and that was simply unacceptable.

With that in mind, I chose to Praise God for the time we had with him.

I used my energy to remember Grayden. I denounced the idea that I would understand His reasons for this and leaned on God to find comfort. I submitted to Him and stopped my intense and potentially endless fight to understand why this happened.

And with this dependency, I gained my freedom.

I was no longer bound to the pain. I stopped fighting with the truth and made the most of the situation.

You commonly hear people saying something might resemble the following, "He would've wanted us to move on without him. He would want us to be happy and love life."

What I realized is that moving on was what I wanted for myself and my family. I wanted us to be happy and love life.

Moving on and loving life again does not diminish his importance to me. Refusing to let his death define our family does not make him less a part of our family.

By embracing what he meant to us and consciously choosing to let our lives continue, we honor not only Grayden, but God's desires for each of us.

In allowing ourselves to depend on God, we gained our independence from the hurt, the pain and the fear of living without him.

Lost my intense
fear of death

And it wasn't because I was ready to die, either.

Maybe it was because I was more focused on getting to heaven. Maybe it was because I finally figured out how to submit to God. Maybe it was a fluke and had no connection at all.

I doubt it.

I had a paralyzing fear of death. It caused me anxiety. It made me uneasy. I would lie still at night and take in the dark and quiet and believe that that was what death would be like. It would cause panic and be completely overwhelming.

Not anymore.

Do I welcome death? Nope. But I no longer fear it.

Something clicked in me and the switch flipped. Death is no longer scary. Death is not an isolation or a separation, it is a reunion.

My situation has changed. Now instead of fearing death, I look forward to heaven.

Felt like he was still going to come around the corner

Was I in denial? Maybe.

His death still didn't seem real…it didn't seem final. There was a large part of me that expected him to bop around the corner and do something to melt our hearts again.

He never did.

I knew he wasn't going to…and yet I still felt like it was going to happen.

I don't remember when that feeling left me. There was not a single moment or happening that led to its demise. It just left me.

I never hoped he would just show up…I did not hope for the impossible. I would've welcomed it, but I knew it was not going to happen. Instead, I just found myself confused at this feeling.

As I struggled with identifying our "new" normal, I couldn't separate Grayden's presence in our old normal. It seemed unnatural, backwards and wrong.

How were we supposed to go back to our lives without him?

I don't believe we weren't supposed to do that at all. It would've been another impossibility. It was impossible because his physical presence did not define his existence in our lives and our memories. He was as much a part of our family now as he ever was. And when I became okay with that, I didn't need him to come around the corner to confirm it.

Got a tattoo

The original idea was a horseshoe shaped magnet with the text "My Boy". That came from my dad, who said Grayden had a magnetic personality and the common phrase I used to greet Grayden when I came home, "How's my boy?"

In talking to the tattoo artist we'd selected, he told us he would recommend someone else for that specific tattoo. As he was a friend of Jamie's from high school, it was important to us that he do the work.

So we shared with him the idea of the Superman logo with a "G" inside accompanied with the saying, "My man of Steele."

I wasn't sold on the idea until our friend, Jamie, who went with us to get a tattoo of her own suggested, "My boy of Steele." When she said that, I knew we had a winner.

Witnessed about 20 of my students show up to his funeral wearing capes they made for him

Somewhere in the middle of the line at the visitation, was a group of my students wearing matching red capes they'd made with a golden "G" outlined on the back. (They made capes for Jamie, Jayce and I as well and we put them on immediately.)

I cannot tell you what this meant to me. I hugged each of them with pride in my heart and tears in my eyes. They'd listened to our request to make this an event a two year old would approve of. They found a way to celebrate Grayden and our family that maybe no one else would appreciate the way I did.

These students were the reason I loved my job, and this show of love and support was exactly what I would've wanted them to learn from me. They thought outside the box, organized and executed a plan and made a statement to their target audience that will never be forgotten. They saw potential and took full advantage of it…and I loved it.

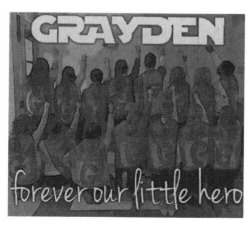

What an amazing gift from an amazing group of students… I miss this crew, they were difference makers.

With the help of a football team, a fraternity and our friends, completed a memorial garden in our front yard

There were a group of young guys from our church that wanted to do something for our family. With the help of one of our friends, who also doubles as a church administrator, we arranged for them to come help us create a memorial garden in the front of our house. They wanted something hands on and interactive and this was something we wanted to make happen anyway…their willingness to help just sped up the process. Additionally, the members of our small group/bible study decided to join the party and the day turned into a full-fledged work day.

My buddy, Adam, and I had already taken out the existing dying bushes and we had planned to build a new border, lay landscaping paper and spread mulch when everyone got to our house. Because we were expecting so many people, we were able to come up with a pretty good list of things that needed to be done: everything from changing batteries in smoke detectors to small painting projects and even some outdoor cleanup and organization.

This crew showed up and everyone got busy…everything on our extremely large list was crossed off except two things—simply amazing.

My mom and dad were in town and we made lunch for everyone—spaghetti and chili with some fixings.

These college guys ate and ended up thanking us for letting them be a part of the day. It seemed completely backwards to me so I told them, "Really guys, we should be the ones thanking you all."

The response I got went something like this, "No, not at all…we will never forget what we were able to do here today. I am so glad we got to know your family and get to see what Grayden was really like. Several of us have worked with him in Journey Kids (our church's nursery program) but now we all feel like we know him. This was truly special."

Watched my brother's basketball team play in the state tournament... and got a t-shirt made

Less than a week after he died, Jamie, Jayce and I made the trek to watch my brother's basketball team play in the state semi-finals. I needed something else to think about and surrounding myself with family and something I enjoy seemed like a no-brainer.

Two of my cousins' kids were on the team—one from my mom's side and one from my dad's side so there were a ton of people there that I knew well.

They drew a tough assignment in the semis, facing the school that won each of the state tournaments the previous year. They were big, strong and athletic... and we knew going in it would be a battle.

Kurt's team had a five point lead at halftime and we liked where we stood. During the halftime break, I walked around the lobby area outside of the gymnasium and stumbled upon a state tournament t-shirt stand—the kind where you could get your name and number on the back.

I had been to several state tournaments but never purchased a t-shirt because of the cost. Something about today was different. I wasn't sold on the idea of getting a shirt personalized, but I was intrigued enough to put some thought into it.

I knew I wanted to include Grayden somehow...and I knew I wanted "Go Uncle Kurt." The number was what I was unsure of. I played around with the idea of "2" because he was two years old, but it didn't speak to me. So I started to play with the idea of "2.5."

When I realized 2 and 5 were the numbers of my cousins' kids, I knew I had a winner.

I approached the t-shirt vendor and told him of the situation and asked if he could somehow manipulate a decimal point. He said he could make it work... and he did.

I immediately put the shirt on and wore it for the second half. Unfortunately, Kurt's team ran out of juice—their opponent was just too deep and I really believe the better team won. I think if they played that team 10 times, they probably lose 8 times. No shame in playing hard and just getting beat.

The good news is, they came back in the third place game and won a convincing decision. All in all, it was a good day. And even though they didn't come home with the big trophy like we all hoped, the third place trophy was bigger than the fourth place trophy.

Watched videos of him

I didn't really need a reason.

Sometimes I just wanted to see him. I wanted to see him be alive and full of life. I wanted to witness his personality and see my normal two year old boy.

Sometimes I wanted to smile because of him. Other times, I needed to cry—I needed the release.

Was I torturing myself? Nope.

There is just something to be said about a physical reminder as opposed to a mental one. When I saw him dancing and singing on a computer screen or television, I didn't have to rely on faith and memory to see him. He was just there.

So much of my train of thought relied upon believing in things I could not see. I discovered comfort in a God I knew was there but did not reveal himself in the physical form--and at times, as I struggled with making sense of a horrid situation, it was exhausting.

I didn't have to believe in a memory when I saw him in front of me. And even though I knew seeing him "alive" again would not return him to us, it didn't matter—that was not what this was about.

It was a temporary escape and it brought me peace. I worked hard and was successful in making sure these videos did not become idols to me because I knew there was danger in that.

They were simply a way for me to see my boy how I wanted to remember him.

Made the phone calls to our family

I called Jamie's sister, Kari, at work first because I needed her to be there for Jamie. I didn't know what the rest of the day was going to look like but I knew our house was full of police, emergency medical technicians, detectives and personnel from the medical examiners' office.

My words were not articulate. I was direct and without the ability to show sensitivity in my delivery—that is one of my biggest regrets to this day. It was the first time in my life that I understood true shock.

I remember telling her I was sorry for calling her at work but that I needed her to come to our house because "Grayden didn't wake up from his nap today." She said, "well, is he okay?" and all I could manage to say was, "no…he's not" That is all I remember about that conversation.

I called my mom next. I remember saying, "Mom, something terrible has happened. I need you to come to St. Louis because Grayden didn't wake up from his nap today."

I remember a pause and hearing my mom say, "Oh, Brent…I am so sorry." I don't remember anything else about that phone call either.

I talked with Jamie's mom next. Then I called my sisters. Then, I was done.

The next two hours, or so, are a blur.

Were those the worst phone calls I've ever had to make? Yes—not even close.

I hope nothing ever changes that.

Sang the same songs to his brother I sang to him

I remember the first time Jayce finished the lines of "Twinkle, Twinkle Little Star." Had I closed my eyes, I would've believed Grayden was in my arms again.

His voice was the same, he whispered it the same way Grayden did when he was tired.

My first instinct was to cry and stop singing—because what I was feeling at the time was gut wrenching. Luckily, I never stopped singing that night...or any night since.

I don't want Jayce to be raised any differently because of Grayden's death. I don't want him to get by with more or less. I don't want him to miss out on anything because of how it makes us feel. I don't want him to be shorted or have more advantage because we cannot appropriately deal with his brother's death.

Not singing to Jayce is simply not an option. Music is a part of me...and I want him to be influenced by it as well.

My nightly routine with Grayden included rocking with and singing to him. It is not fair to Jayce that he not get that same thing because I am unable to handle the way it makes me feel.

I made the decision that night that I would not let pain and sadness affect my decision-making when it came to Jayce's upbringing. Did I struggle with it from time to time? Did I tear up occasionally? I sure did...and you know what? That is okay.

Jayce is the trump card to pain: a reminder that I am still a father...and I love being a father.

Watched something go viral in his honor

We asked our family and friends not to wear black to the funeral. We wanted the service to be something that, if it were not a funeral, and if he were here to be a part of it, would be something that he would enjoy. We asked people to wear bright colors, super hero shirts—anything that would be acceptable to a two year old.

What happened next was awesome.

A friend of mine from college changed her facebook photo to a cartoon character. She then went public with the idea for others to do so as well.

This was then picked up by more of my friends…and they did the same.

I know of over two hundred people who changed their pictures for our little man. This number includes friends, family members, fraternity brothers, college professors, church members, former teachers, colleagues, former students and people we don't even know.

I got messages from people four degrees away-- "I am a friend of a mother to a student of a fraternity brother of yours." A friend of a friend of a friend.

People made these changes and published the reason. They said his name… they told his story and it touched people.

Put together a choir to sing for him

It started with a simple request:

Culver Choir alums...if you are in the St. Louis area and are available to come celebrate the life of our Grayden, please join us at the church Thursday at 11:00 to help send him off in style. I need as many voices as I can to make joyful noise for the lord in honor of our boy. We will be singing "In the Upper Room" loud enough for everyone to hear it. We will try to find a room to run it at 10:30. Please respond to this if you are able and willing.

What it led to was 76 responses and a choir of 32 to sing Grayden home. I am humbled by some of the responses I received...

"Brent, I am absolutely heart broken to hear about your precious son!!! I WISH I could be there, I'd do it in a heartbeat! :(lifting you and your family in prayers!!!

"I have to work, or else you know I'd truly be there. What an awesome thing you're doing for your son!"

"I'll be singing the soprano line from Canada and thinking of you and your sweet little dude."

"That is perfect, Brent. I'm so sorry I can't be there, but I pray you have an overwhelming amount of voices!"

"I'm unable to be there, but my heart will be full of songs for you."

"I'm able and willing. Be there at 10:30 it is very close to my work."

"I'll be there and ready to make a joyful noise to the Lord! I'm taking the day off, so let me know if you need help with anything else that morning or the rest of the day."

"Wish I could be there...that was always one of my favorite songs...my thoughts are with you."

"Wish I could be there to sing with you all."

"I will be there for sure. Love you guys so very much."

"I will be singing for him from Indiana as I will unfortunately be unable to attend."

"Brent, if I had the time available from work, I would be there in a heartbeat. What a fitting tribute to your son and the Lord that has called him home. Always my favorite song that we sang as a choir. My thoughts and prayers are with you and your family during this time."

"What a great song. I will be singing it from Ohio. God bless you and your family."

"I will truly be there with you in spirit, as we share in the Holy Spirit as brothers and sisters in Christ. I will stop at 11am Thursday to sing here at home."

"I am seeing if I can make it work. Want to hug you and Jamie and sing with you. Your faith in the Lord is evident. It is truly inspirational. Love you so much:)"

"Wish I could be there to sing it with you in person big guy. My heart goes out to you and your family, Brent. I will be singing it with you, just from Iowa... What a beautiful tribute that I wish I could share with you! Many prayers are being sent from my family to yours brother!"

"I'll be there!!!! . . . Now to find a Wonder Woman shirt:)"

"Hey buddy, if I were home this week, I'd be there. I'll make sure that I'm there in spirit at the given time. You're in my prayers and thoughts. I can't begin to image what you're dealing with. God is working through this in ways you may never see."

"Been praying for you since I saw your post last night--so sorry for your loss. If Tulsa was a closer drive, I'd love to stand and sing with you!!"

"Brent, I'd be honored if you still need singers."

"I wish I could be with you to sing, but I will be praising God and singing with you in heart. I love you and your family. God is good!"

When we gathered before the funeral to do a quick run-through, I shared with everyone the importance of this song. Several of our friends from St. Louis agreed to sing with us and it was important they knew the many levels to which this song spoke to me.

I explained to everyone that this particular song was a song I first heard my freshman year of college at Culver-Stockton College. I went on to say that in my many years of choral music, this was my favorite song I'd ever performed.

Every year we took a week long choir tour and we ended every concert singing this benediction. Its melody is sweet and serene and the harmonies bring tears to my eyes every time I hear it.

Our choir, like many other collegiate groups, shared a special bond. There was a certain amount of pride that was associated with being a member, amongst its members.

This was the second time I had arranged for a choir to perform this song at a function for our family. We did the same thing at our wedding just over six years prior. It was my gift to Jamie.

Additionally and potentially most importantly, I sang this song to both of my boys as I rocked with them during our bedtime routine. It was my favorite lullaby and I knew when Grayden would hear it, that he would recognize it.

The message of the song was simple, "Children I am with you but a little while, where I go, you cannot follow. You will seek but will not find me, but you know that I am the way."

To send Grayden to be with God with this particular song, was the perfect final lullaby for my boy.

Grayden on his
first birthday.

Spent 6 and a half hours at his visitation

The death of a child is something that speaks to people. This is evidenced by the fact that we spent six and a half hours with a line full of people coming to show us love. Our friends told us there was a solid two hour wait. The folks from our gigantic funeral home told us it was the largest visitation they'd ever had.

When a child dies, people recognize it as a terrible thing. It hits close to home to every parent and grandparent. The show of support we received was outstanding.

The challenge is being a presence once the newness wears off. Once life resumes and those not directly affected move on, those grieving still hurt.

Heard a song I thought was written for me to hear

Music speaks to me. But it has never spoken to me like this.

Less than a week after the funeral, we were heading to Jamie's parents to meet up with her grandparents and some of her other family. I needed to drive separately and on my way, Jamie called me to see if I would stop and pick up the pizzas they'd ordered. As it was on my way, it was not a big deal at all.

When I pulled in the parking lot, a song came on the Christian radio station that caught my attention.

It opened with just the piano and there was something about the melody that was hypnotizing to me. I was immediately drawn in. When the vocals began, I heard a tenor voice saying, "I'm tired, I'm worn, my heart is heavy" At this point I was hooked.

The chorus revealed the following: Let me see redemption win, let me know the struggle ends, that you can mend a heart that's frail and torn. I want to know a song can rise, from the ashes of a broken life, when all that's dead inside has been reborn…I'm worn."

After the completion of the song, another song immediately came on and I did not get either title or artist. Knowing I wanted to hear it again, I sent Jamie a text that simply said, "I'm worn…Let me see redemption win" I wanted the reminder in my phone so I could make sure I could find it again…at that point, I had no clue if it was a song that was ten years old or brand new.

I learned shortly after that that the song was a new release from the band Tenth Avenue North entitled, "Worn." I loved it…I listened to it repeatedly and I felt like it spoke to me.

Months later, when I heard that Tenth Avenue North was coming to St. Louis, I was pretty pumped and wanted to go…specifically to hear that song. Unfortunately, they were going to be at Six Flags and tickets, with the price of admission to the park were just not in the cards. We talked about it, but just couldn't make it happen.

Fast forward about six more months.

I heard an advertisement for Winter Jam. It was a concert featuring ten popular Christian artists. I recognized 8 of the ten performers and was most excited to see Tenth Avenue North on the docket.

The day of the concert, I had completely forgotten about the show. Luckily for me, some friends of ours came over after lunch to watch the football playoff game and said they were going to this concert. When they asked me if I wanted to go, they didn't have to spend too much time talking me into it. Boy, was I ever glad I decided to go.

It was a great concert, highlighted by the band I wanted to see most. "Worn" was the third song they played. It began with the lead singer belting out the chorus a capella. It gave me chills. I was emotional all day and this melody set me free. Tears filled my eyes as I was overcome with emotion.

At the end of the initial chorus, the piano continued as the lead singer spoke to the audience. He said, "I want everyone here to put their hands in the air. I ask you to do this, not as if to say, 'we are Christians, look at us.' I ask you to do this because this is what a child does when they want their daddy to pick them up."

With that message, I wanted more than anything to pick up my boy. I wanted him to want that from me—to pick him up.

Instead, I cried. Hard.

I sobbed uncontrollably…unbridled, passionate and without hesitation. My buddy, Adam, was thankfully there to hold me up.

I needed that cry. I needed that release.

I hate that I was not able to sing along like I'd hoped to, but hearing that song live really spoke to me.

It represented my previous year. I was both tired and worn. My heart was heavy and I needed to know God would restore me. Appropriately enough (and in tune with the lyrics) I found that message in a song…in this song.

Found my strength in the moon

I cannot tell you how many times I received texts or e-mailed pictures of the moon. Dozens of times...really.

The message at his funeral was simple, but profound. Its effect on people is immeasurable.

The basis is simple: We know the moon is round, we've seen it—we have visual proof. During the day, the moon is not visible, but we still know it to be round. In all stages of the moon, it does not appear to be a full circle, but we know that it is.

God's love is illustrated in this precise picture--Even though we cannot see God's love, we know it exists. In saying, "The moon is round," what I am reminded of is God's presence in my life.

I get a nudge when I struggle to recognize God's grace. I find comfort in the recognition that I am not alone in this. I breathe easier because my anxiety is no longer overwhelming.

Every time I see the moon, I am comforted.

I remember that Grayden is being cared for by God, and I find contentment in this truth.

Sang at a funeral... our first since his

The Reeds are an extended part of our family. Carol was my kindergarten teacher, Shelley and Darcy were my babysitters. I used to watch Michael and Tyler. Lee and Carol are two of my parents' best friends. The connections are not limited to just that either.

They are a family that was always with us. I cannot remember a time when they were not a close part of our lives. My boys called them Grandma Carol and Papa Lee.

When I got the call saying Lee's cancer had come back, it did not make for a good day.

Having recently lost Grayden, I was not ready to deal with this, too. And although the two situations were not comparable, the news left me feeling sad and disappointed—two feelings I had become familiar with.

When Lee died, I got the call from Grandma Carol.

I was reminded of the first phone call I made to someone who wasn't a blood family member the day we lost Grayden. I dialed a number I'd known by heart since I was probably six years old and heard a familiar voice on the other end say, "Hello." I noticed it was shaky and I sensed it came from someone who had been crying. My simple response was, "Hi Grandma Carol."

That day we cried together. This day we would too.

She'd called to ask me to sing at the funeral, citing her concerns that it might be too much for me. She gave me an out and let me know everyone would understand if the timing just wasn't right.

Not singing at his funeral was not an option—so long as that is what they wanted from me.

At the time I had sang in 95 weddings and 36 funerals. There is something humbling about getting to be a part of these ceremonies. There is something special about being a part of the beginning of a new union and life together.

There is something profound about being able to be a part of the celebration of a person's life.

Did I expect it to be difficult? Yup.

Did it matter? Not one bit.

This day would be difficult no matter what. But I had an opportunity. I had an opportunity to provide some healing through music. I believe it does that… not because of me, but because of what a message in music can communicate.

This would be the third funeral I'd sung for this family. The first was Carol's mother. The second was Michael's.

Michael died when he was in his early twenties. It was unexpected and unprovoked…much like Grayden's. Michael and I always shared a special connection. I looked out for him and I know I was important to him, too.

When I talked to Carol about songs for Lee's service, she selected a song with a special message that helped her deal with Michael's death and a song that I sang at Michael's funeral.

In what would make this particular song even more meaningful to me, I would be singing it with Darcy, Lee and Carol's daughter. We worked it up and it was perfect.

I made it through each song without any unnecessary emotional responses. I sang what I felt were strong songs.

When I wasn't singing, I wept.

I wept for the family. I wept because I missed Grayden. I wept because even though Lee was in heaven, he wouldn't be there the next time I stopped by.

I had a much better understanding of death following Grayden's, but that didn't help me to like it any more.

Singing at Lee's funeral was necessary for me. I needed to "get back on the horse," so to speak. What better way is there to do that than paying tribute to a man you respected and loved, with his family sitting in the front row?

Nothing about Lee's death had anything to do with Grayden. But there was something about it that everyone allowed to be handled simultaneously for our sake. We shared pain and got through each together.

It was a reminder of death, and we hated that. I suspect death will always be sad. And even though I will certainly always equate death with sadness, that will not be the only thing it will inspire.

The good news is, it is also a reminder of the joy of salvation and the promise of heaven, and we love that.

Told stories about him

Every chance I could. And then, I told them again—often times to the same people.

You know, I never got the feeling people were listening merely because they pitied our situation. They always seemed to be genuinely interested in what I had to say about him.

Telling these stories maintained a connection to him. It kept him alive. It reminded me I was his daddy and that I was proud of him.

Sharing his stories, and my pride, is what I would've done if he were still with us. I want people to know my boy…and while I am not afraid I will forget him, I would rather actively remember him than be content with keeping those memories to myself.

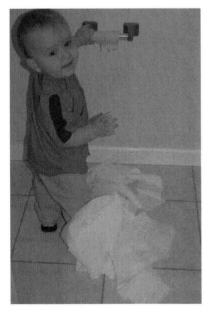

Ironically, this was not the first,
(nor the last) time this happened.

Knocked out a professional boxer in a boxing match

Okay, so it was in Wii boxing, but I am counting it. And you would too, she was undefeated in her boxing career!

It was a game night with friends…a regularity at our house. We often tell people, "We are young and broke, do you want to come and be young and broke with us?"

This was the first time after we lost him that I felt real and normal again. For about three hours I didn't think about anything other than having fun with our friends. It was a nice escape…and I don't even think escape is an accurate term. Our evening was not devoid of him…just the sadness we associated with his passing at the time.

We laughed hard and felt normal…and you better believe I will tell anyone who asks that I knocked out a professional boxer.

Was given hope by a three year old

On our way to a grief counseling appointment, I had an impromptu conversation with a three year old, one of Grayden's buddies, Blaise:

Blaise: "Hi...Where's Grayden? ...Where's Grayden? ...Where's Grayden?"

Me: "Well, he's not with us"

Blaise: "Where is he?"

Me: "Um, well...he's in heaven"

Blaise: "Why's he in heaven?"

Jamie (because I begin to struggle a bit): "Because Jesus needed him to come there and spend some time with him."

Blaise (with very little hesitation): "Oh...just like my daddy"

And instantly, the twinge of sadness I felt was gone because of the beauty and the innocence of the mind of a three year old...Thanks, Blaise...I appreciate that, buddy!

Blaise, Luke and Grayden at
his second birthday party

Struggled when I thought about baseball, fishing and math homework

Grayden working on his casting skills

Grayden in his Cardinal red

When I thought about the future, I felt empty. I looked forward to teaching him so many things. I reveled in the potential and couldn't wait to see his response.

There were several things I hated that I would not get to experience with him.

I hated the idea of missing his prom, his wedding and his graduations. I hated to miss potty training, sledding and camping. I hated not being able to experience teaching him to drive, how to treat a woman and how to get along with his brother.

To be honest, for a while, I hated just about everything. Anything that resembled potential lost, I hated it. I felt shorted and I was angry and bitter.

Of all the things that bothered me, there were three that really seemed to stick out: baseball, fishing and math homework.

Math homework? Really?

Maybe it was because I was good with numbers and I knew that would be my responsibility. Maybe it was because it was one of the first things I thought of and I just couldn't get it out of my mind. I wouldn't get to teach him multiplication or talk him through division…but why did that bother me? I have racked my brain to try to figure this one out…and to no avail. This seems to just be one of those things I am hung up on. Not a big deal…probably something that will always make me chuckle just a bit.

Baseball and fishing, though? I think I could make some sense out of those. Here is where I was:

I wasn't going to get to take him to t-ball practice or coach his little league team. There wouldn't be anymore Cardinals games. There would be no jerseys or razzing our family members who liked the Cubs. I wouldn't be able to play catch with my boys in the backyard…and there wouldn't be any "hot box" either. How can you play a game that takes three people with only two?

I wasn't going to be able to dig for night crawlers and clean fish with him. There wouldn't be ice fishing in the winter months and I wouldn't get to take his picture holding the first fish he ever caught? I would never have to remind him to be quiet because it would scare the fish away.

So why these things?

My best guess is that baseball and fishing were things I shared with my dad. They were the things I looked forward to with Grayden because they were our quality family time activities when I was a kid. I don't remember fishing with my mom and I don't remember playing catch with her either. I am sure that I did at some point, but the way I remember it, that was something that was a sacred event between a father and son. That is how I coded it.

Will I think of him every time I do these activities with his brother? Probably… at least for a moment. And I find no fault in that. Will I let it haunt me and thwart my ability to enjoy these things without him? Absolutely not. I have no time for that.

Do you think I will hope there are good fishing holes and a pair of ball gloves when I get to heaven? Yup.

The brilliant part about this scenario is, I know once I get to heaven, it will not matter.

Found a pretzel in a Band-Aid box

Actually, my wife did.

This was a couple months after he left us. Boy, did we need it, too.

It was as simple as a pretzel in a band-aid box on the surface—but it was so much more than that. It was a reminder that he can still make us smile…and that that is okay. We thanked him for that and chuckled at the gift he gave us: an illustration of innocence and a reminder of a regular life.

At that time, we had no idea what normal was going to look like…and some days, we still struggle with that. However, when that pretzel showed up in that Band-Aid box, we were a normal family again with normal issues…struggling at bedtime, having toys all over the floor and finding things in crazy places.

Grayden's gift to us that day was brilliant—a reminder that even though nothing felt normal and everything was out of sorts, something as simple as a pretzel in a Band-Aid box humbled us and allowed us to remember real-life things still happen. It was a subtle reminder that we were going to be okay.

Went to the movies with my family... without him

*Went to the movies today with some of my nieces and nephews--saw "The Croods."
It was tough to not have little man with us but we tried to ease that struggle with
a big thing of popcorn and pop (It's pop, not soda). This is important because I
am usually too cheap to buy those things--thanks grandma and grandpa for co-
sponsoring this event!!*

*I am glad to get the first trip to the movies with kids out of the way...only a few
teary moments and now we can cross that off the list of firsts. I could hear him
saying, "wow" and "whoa, daddy."*

*The movie theater is a place Grayden and I never made it to...although I am
convinced he would've love it as much as I do. We'd planned to hit the dollar
theater to see "Wreck it Ralph" but that was just not in the plans. He loved "his
shows," for sure.*

I prefer to think there is a giant movie screen in heaven with a crisp, clear
picture and super cool surround sound - and that makes me smile.

The family at "Frozen"
...our first Christmas without him

Realized his death had nothing to do with me

I was devastated. I was irrational. I was selfish.

And in accordance with those thoughts, I reacted appropriately. I remember saying in one of our counseling sessions, "God, you had my attention. I was trying to submit. You didn't have to do this. I would've listened."

I was stuck in this horrid place where I needed to understand. And like I do, I blamed myself. I could completely understand that. If this was my fault, I could learn to deal with it and move on...at some point.

Our counselor responded by saying something that I believe was not only appropriate, but also spot on.

"What if Grayden's death had nothing to do with you?"

I had no response.

He went on to say that God's plan was much bigger than just me.

I felt a sense of relief and a release of guilt almost immediately. My irrational, selfish devastation led me to blame myself for something I had no control over. I needed to hurt...I was selfish in that manner. And selfishness is not always a negative thing. But I did not need to be stuck in a place in which everything was my fault. When it was presented to me, I was able to accept it.

This was an important part of my healing process. It is most comfortable for me to blame myself when I encounter hardship. But this time, it didn't add up.

God was not punishing me for something I did or didn't do. Maybe, he wasn't even punishing me at all.

Worried about how to best care for my family

And I still do.

It is important to me to be a good father and husband.

I take pride in the opportunity I have to lead my family. The unfortunate truth is, right now, I am called to lead them through something I wish we were not facing.

I suspect this will continue to be a work in progress—and I am okay with that.

My focus will continue to be, to do the best I can. Listen, learn and live. This is not an issue of pass or fail. It is more of an issue of survive and thrive. I look forward to the time when our sole focus is thrive.

Received random things in the mail

I wrote the following on several different days...

"Got a nice, unexpected pick-me-up today.

A package arrived from Amazon...and neither Jamie nor I had ordered anything. When I opened it, I found an awesome crescent moon birdfeeder for Grayden's memorial garden.

A friend of ours here in the Lou put a picture of it on facebook and Jamie commented on how freaking awesome it was. The message at Grayden's funeral was, "The moon is round" --We know this to be true whether we can physically see it or not...just like God and his love for us.

The birdfeeder came with a note from a friend of mine back home. Her family is important to me (love the whole Markey gang) and I sang at her and her husband's wedding.

I want to thank Wes and Hannah Moss...and their kids Loralei and Kiptyn for really brightening our day.

On a rainy day when it is hard to get excited, this really made a difference and I am so thankful for this simple act.

We are blessed to have family and friends that continue to think of us and pray for us. I miss my boy constantly and consistently...and even though things are getting easier to manage, there is still consistent pain and emptiness. The random texts, messages and surprises we continue to receive help us in ways I cannot even explain.

I am excited about being able to pay this forward...thanks!"

"Just got a package in the mail from one of my best friends who lives in Orlando now...thanks Jenn Huffman for the additions to Grayden's garden! I bet you all can figure out which came from the land of the magic kingdom. I have stories about our little guy with Mickey and Pooh, both...such an amazing addition. We love how our friends and family love us..."

"The newest member of the memorial garden is "Chief"

...this is a gift from some friends of ours in Kansas City. Zach and Kari have a special connection to Grayden, their son was born on the same day."

He looks great...like he belongs there...thanks, Team Gibb!

"Continue to be picked up when we do not expect it. A friend of ours sent us a package today that arrived in the mail. When I opened it, I found a 42 page scrapbook full of images of our family. It was beautiful and perfect.

It oozed with personality, just like our little guy.

Thank you Peggy Williams, you truly made our day!

Peggy owns the Scrapbook Nook in Colchester, IL and I got to know her well in grad school through my friend, Jarrah. What a great gift this was that came on a day when our house is dealing with a nasty bug."

Looked out the window and saw a tornado

Jamie, Jayce and I went to our friends' Adam and Kaitlin's house for dinner one evening. The original plan was to have dinner, put Jayce down, and play some games.

Our plan, however, took a turn with the arrival of the tornado sirens.

Luckily for us, they have a basement. After about three minutes down there, Adam decided, "If I am going to be stuck down here, at least I am going to do something productive…I am going upstairs to get a load of laundry."

Being equally antsy, and curious about what the sky looked like, I decided I couldn't stay downstairs either. I announced to the group, "I am not going to let him die by himself, I am going up to help him."

When I got to the top of the stairs, I asked him if he had everything and snuck a look out the window, expecting to see absolutely nothing. That is not what I saw.

The window was filled with a black "V"

I remember saying, "Um, Adam, there is a tornado—right there."

His response was immediate, "Get downstairs, right now."

We got back down to where the girls and Jayce were and told them what we'd seen. From there, we spent about 45 minutes in a small closet…waiting.

As we closed the door, we said a quick prayer and enjoyed the time the best way we could.

I would be lying if I said I did not want to go upstairs and look. However, I did resist. I couldn't leave my family alone. The idea that we might be in danger did not cause any excess anxiety, but I recognized its presence.

It's funny, because I remember feeling more adrenaline than fear. It was a bizarre rush and I never felt like anything bad was going to happen—even after seeing the funnel cloud directly outside the window.

I watched my child, completely clueless of any impending danger, explore this small closet and charm the four of us. We told stories, reminisced and waited… together.

There was a sense of togetherness that night that we had been craving. Grayden wasn't with us, but our family seemed together.

Facing a potentially scary situation, I wasn't scared.

Perhaps I carried with me the idea that Grayden was watching over us. Maybe I was okay with the idea that the result might be our reunion in the place I most wanted to go. What if, for the first time since we lost him, I didn't have time to miss him or feel fear because my family needed my focus to be elsewhere.

I don't think it matters, I would take any of those reasons and be okay with it.

Learned to accept help...
at least a little bit more

We were blessed with an amazing support system. People wanted to help us. Everywhere we looked, and even those places we did not, people were searching for ways to help our family.

Families sent us checks because they wanted to support us. Groups of people came to our house to help with chores.

For every person who was afraid to talk to us, there were two who wanted to help us.

However, there was a problem with that—at least initially. We didn't know how to ask for help, and we felt awkward and unworthy when accepting it.

A new friend of mine put it best. He is a Chiropractor who heard of our story and sought me out. I knew of him through a mutual friend and got word that he wanted to treat me and would not charge me for his services.

I was humbled and appreciative, but something in me was keeping me from taking advantage of this amazing gift.

After a couple weeks, he contacted me. He broke the ice, verbalized the awkwardness and invited me to come in to see if he would be able to help me. He asked me to let him help me…and I accepted.

I remember my second visit. Doc had done the initial evaluation and I had returned to the office to talk about my treatment plan. He pointed out some things he believed he could help me with and then made the transition to payment. The conversation was simple and direct—and was exactly what I needed.

He told me he understood financial hardship, citing his first year out of Chiropractic school. He told me about how he was unable to find a position and his wife, who was a nurse, was only able to find a part-time position. I listened to him tell me how they lived off of $14,000 that year.

He told me he "got it." Said that educated individuals were supposed to be able to make money for their families, but sometimes it just wasn't God's plan for them at that particular time.

I will never forget what he told me next.

He said, "Look, man, I am sure you prayed for God to provide for you, to help you. And this is how he is doing it…so I want you to let me help you."

And I did.

Went yard-saling

When I was young, I loved to yard sale with my mom. It was our quality family-time activity. It is how I learned to read a map—mom would give me the map and the list of addresses and say, "Okay, get us to the next one"

I love a bargain, thrive on finding a good deal and consider myself frugal… others might say cheap (and they are right). I don't see the point in wasting money and do my best to stretch a dollar as far as it will go.

One particular Saturday, one of my former students had come for a weekend visit. We decided to hit some yard sales to see if we could find anything we couldn't live without. The first sale we stopped at, we hit the proverbial yard sale jackpot.

I found a Little Tikes ride-on toy, a jeep, for $10. It needed a new battery but I'd priced one and knew I could pick one up without much trouble. As I was loading it up, the gentleman hosting the sale said to me, "I've got a four wheeler back there, too if you are interested in it?" I asked him what he wanted for it and he said, "I don't know, ten bucks" Without hesitation, I bought it, too.

Two major scores…and only twenty bucks in—nice!

I caught myself thinking, the boys are going to love these…and then I stopped breathing as I remembered Grayden wouldn't get to experience this. The twinge of disappointment lasted just seconds and I thought of how much fun it would be for Jayce to ride these with a friend, while Grayden watched from above.

Although I have always been drawn to a good deal, my wife had made it clear to me that I needed to be aware of what I brought home from yard sales. I contemplated briefly this double purchase knowing that if Grayden were still with us, this would be a no-brainer. Part of me wanted to buy it just because I would've had he not died…but I knew I could not make decisions based purely on hypotheticals. Instead, I made the purchase with the belief that it would bring Jayce and his friends joy. My decision was confirmed when I found the exact toys I purchased originally priced at a total of $620. There is certainly value there.

The value of the purchase was undeniable. The value of his brother, Jayce, laughing and having fun is immeasurable. I look forward to seeing kids drive these, like Jayce and Grayden would've. I find joy in the idea that Jayce can play with his friends like he would've his brother. I am saddened in knowing I will not witness my boys experiencing this on earth, but I refuse to let that stop me from doing things I enjoy...especially when they will bring joy to my family.

Something as simple as a "major score" at a yard sale might seem unimportant to you, but to me, it is a way to feel normal when everything else seems unstable. Don't underestimate the importance of the little things in the healing process.

Found my bucket list and challenged myself to cross 10 things off in 10 days

1. Sleep in a tent with Jocelyn, Alison, Luke, Nico, Ethan and Caitlin

2. Have a great idea and get t-shirts made because of it

3. Write a catchy tune

4. Play Lincoln Logs with Jayce

5. Get a book published

6. Throw a New Year's Rockin' Eve costume party

7. Eat an entire tootsie roll flavored tootsie pop without biting it

8. Hit a quick

9. Drive a four speed 1981 Ford Escort one more time

10. Buy a minivan

11. Play beer pong with my dad...bizarre, I know

12. Play hockey with Ethan

13. Build a snowman with a little girl that looks just like Jamie

14. Dress up like Matt Foley-Motivational Speaker one year for Halloween

15. Donate something that will save someone's life

16. Do something that takes somebody's breath away

17. Wear a leisure suit

18. Have a martini...in Seattle...but I am not eating the olive...I don't even want the olive in the drink

19. Hear Grayden say my name

20. Jump in one of those inflatable jumpy things

21. Get my picture taken with someone in one of those little booths at the mall

22. See the Eiffel Tower with Jamie

23. Sing karaoke with my grandma

24. Learn to say words in 10 different languages

25. Go to Panama

26. See a real cobra...but not at a zoo

27. Kiss someone's mommy under the mistletoe

28. Meet Adam Pascal or Idina Menzel

29. Teach a parrot to say something my nieces and nephews would get in trouble for

30. Adopt a bulldog puppy

31. Go ice skating with Caitlin

32. Cook a seven-course meal from scratch and share it with someone

33. Hear Pearl Jam live

34. Pitch to Luke

35. Paint my face and go to a soccer match

36. Get a tattoo I designed myself

37. Wake up in a foreign country

38. Meet someone whose names begin with a Q and a Z in the same day

39. Play volleyball with Jocelyn

40. Go on an all-inclusive vacation with at least four friends

41. Experience the Great Barrier Reef up close and personal

42. Swim with Alison

43. Build a wiffleball field with a homerun fence in my back yard

44. See The Nutcracker...because I got hosed in fourth grade

45. Drink a Blue Moon with Greg

46. Eat chocolate covered strawberries

47. Dress up like the Easter Bunny

48. Volunteer at a soup kitchen on a major holiday

49. Go to New York City for a week and see a different Broadway show every night

50. Sleep under the stars and wake up with someone in my arms

51. Go to that theme park in Ohio and ride every roller coaster

52. Witness Illinois beat Iowa in person again

53. Catch a big game fish in the ocean

54. Take Noah to see a real elephant

55. Have a Star Wars Marathon and watch all six movies in one sitting... and I'm not even that big of a fan

56. Go to a movie premiere

57. Eat french fries in a Chinese Restaurant

58. Play Twister

59. Dance close to a girl that smells really good and sing in her ear

60. Build a piece of furniture out of legos

61. Get a facial

62. Attend a World Series game

63. Two words…ear candles

64. Start a card club

65. Eat a goldfish

66. Paint with Nico

67. Do a load of laundry and have no stray socks

68. Eat sushi

69. Marry Jamie

70. Get a massage

71. Jump off a cliff into some sort of body of water

72. Do a craft with Ava

73. Go to a surprise party for me!

74. Sing with a live band

75. Decorate a Clark W. Griswold-type house at Christmastime

76. Be an extra in a movie

77. Tickle Kaleigh and then listen to one of her short stories

78. Swim with dolphins

79. Create a 200 foot slip 'n slide and ride the whole thing

80. Sell a painting

81. Sit in the audience for Saturday Night Live

82. Watch a horse being born

83. Learn how to curl...easy, it's an Olympic sport

84. Be on the news for something legal

85. Make rice krispie treats with Hunter

86. Learn how to make peanut butter

87. Paint a Disney Villains bathroom

88. Throw a football with Jacob

89. Play tennis on a clay court and a grass court

90. Do a flip on a trampoline

91. Watch Luke win a wrestling match or have an assist and score a goal in the same game

92. Drink a gallon of milk in a half hour without vomiting

93. Eat homemade ice cream with Andrew

94. Jump off the top rope in a professional wrestling ring

95. Shoot par at a putt putt course

96. Take Emily to a movie

97. Call in to Dr. Laura

98. Make a huge snow fort big enough to walk around in

99. Throw a costume party for no particular reason

100. Invent a delicious drink

So…did I succeed in my quest to cross 10 things off in 10 days? Nope—I only got to 8. But it gives me something to shoot for and highlights that life isn't over yet. When I read this list, I laugh and I dream—two of my favorite things to do.

Having something in front of you to represent your hopes, dreams and desires is a great way to combat the overwhelming grief that has a tendency to consume you. I have completed 39 (up to 45, now!) of my hundred items, which means I've got a ton of things left to do. Coolest part of that is, I actually updated this list about six years ago…my original list is probably 2/3 complete by now.

If you don't have a list, I would recommend you make one…and start crossing things off. When you complete the list, make another one!

Watched my nieces and nephews struggle with his death

The first time they were all together

...tie and Grayden, she could never get enough of him.

When Luke first met Grayden, he said when he was 16 he was going to "take him to the store and buy him stuff." When 8-year-old Luke was asked what he was going to buy him, he said, "Whatever he wants."

Death changes families—at every level.

My sisters' kids adored Grayden. When he came to us, it had been almost 7 years since there had been a baby around. Grayden was loved by his cousins, that is for sure. We used to joke that we didn't have to worry about him falling and getting hurt when we were at my parents' house—we were sure if he fell he would fall on someone.

Grayden had his first seizure at my parents house at Christmas—and everybody saw it. My parents, siblings and their spouses and all five of his cousins—ranging in age from 7 to 10. That was a horrifying day for our family. The kids were noticeably upset and scared...and so was I.

When Grayden died, it hit them hard.

My niece Alison insisted on talking to me that night. It was my intention to say the things she needed to hear to be comforted. But through her tears, she was able to accomplish that for me.

They were proud of him...and I didn't realize how much until we lost him.

Catie wrote a report about Grayden, and she got an A+ on it. She has adopted an intense liking of the Teenage Mutant "Engine" Turtles and wears her Turtles shirts all the time. She even dedicates her hockey games to Grayden. Catie informed her mom that she wants to come to St. Louis to visit for a week every summer...we can't wait to have her.

Luke, in his own way, lets us know he was hurting, too. My sister told me that Luke asked, "Mom, who do you think cried the most when Grayden died?" My sister said she was unsure how to respond but quickly heard Luke say, "I think it was me." Grayden used to follow Luke around and we have tons of pictures of the two of them together.

Ethan doesn't usually say too much but I saw him really struggle to pick out pictures of Grayden. He really wanted to make sure he selected the right one.

He used to carry Grayden around and would say things like, "Mom, you know I am going to want to hold him when we get to grandma and grandpa's."

Alison now collects Superman shirts. She loves babies and has a natural gift as a caregiver. She was never afraid to jump right in and change a dirty diaper, give him a bath or do whatever he needed. She would've made any sacrifice necessary to come see my boys and I adored that.

Alison and Grayden at Halloween

Jocelyn posted something on Facebook that broke my heart. There was a period where people would give out numbers and you were asked to share that number of things about yourself that not everyone knows about you. Jocelyn, a teenager who should be worrying about stupid boys, shopping and sports games, thought that one of the most 7 important things people should know about her was that she "thinks about and misses Grayden every day." I love that this is important to her and hate that is even an option all at the same time.

I hate that they have to think about this. But, the truth is, this is our reality. Death happens to adults and children alike. Talk to the children it effects and listen to what they have to say.

This was the first day Jocelyn met Grayden. I still maintain they looked a lot alike.

I was shocked Ethan wanted to hold him at all, and he always fought to hold him first.

Our first Christmas with Grayden

And our first without him…

Went on my first float trip

I'd always wanted to go on a float trip but had never been able to do it.

In college, I was always on choir tour during spring break and was never able to make one right after school let out—there was always something that kept me from going.

When a former student of mine invited Jamie and I to go floating with her family, we made it work.

Jamie was shocked I'd never been and it happened to be on a weekend we had free. That in itself was a small wonder because we were booked pretty solid for the first five months after he died.

When we got there, we met the family. I was immediately comfortable with them because they reminded me of my own family. They seemed to really enjoy being together. They were fun and interactive and the evening was full of stories and reminiscence. We played games and I legitimately felt like I'd known them for years.

They asked us about Grayden.

They seemed reluctant to ask and, I think, were a bit surprised at our willingness to talk about him. They quickly learned that we had no issues sharing our journey. We talked about the hard parts and we talked about learning how to do things a bit better.

We cried with them and had a great time. Like many others, they thanked us for sharing our boy, citing that even though they'd never met him, that they felt like they knew him.

He was easy to talk about and we loved him with everything we had. That is a pretty good combination when you want to accurately and passionately portray someone.

Oh yeah…the actual float trip was awesome, too.

Went to my grandma's 90th birthday party

Our family is close. When Grandpa died, everyone was there and we spent three or four days together.

Grandma's 90th birthday party was our first family event after Grayden died. It was good to see everyone, and even though my sister and a couple of my cousins were absent, the most glaring omission to me was the void left by Grayden's absence.

I excused myself a couple times and spent some time swinging on the playground outside. Mostly I just sat on the swing. I wanted to be with everyone, but something kept me from doing that.

I allowed myself a moment and then realized that even though Grandma would've been okay with me excusing myself, that it would break my heart if she knew I was struggling—because it would break hers to know I was hurting.

I got myself together, put on a fake smile, headed straight to the cake table and did the best I could to not be awkward and uncomfortable.

I really was thrilled to be there with all the people I grew up with and adore my grandma…that was not fake. There was something about this first family get together without him that elevated his absence.

The majority of the Harper cousins at
Grandma's 90th birthday party

The worst part of the day was posing for our first family picture without him… it nearly killed me. But, we did it and from that point on, it was not as big a deal because it had already happened at least once…I am thankful for that.

The best part of the day was seeing Grandma smile…hugging her multiple times and being able to kiss her as I told her "happy birthday." Those conversations tend to happen over the phone these days.

There were some tears, because some members of our family had not yet been able to mourn with us. It was yet another bittersweet moment in a year chalked full of them.

I remember feeling three things that day: sadness that he was not there, guilt that my inability to separate my emotions potentially detracted from Grandma's day and love.

Even though I can still talk about the first two, the love is what I remember the most.

Gave a community church service

I grew up in small-town Illinois – Blandinsville, to be exact. Approximately 800 people. You could ride your bike anywhere you wanted when you were a kid. I loved the small town life—still do.

Every year, we have our town celebration, The Farmers Picnic. It is complete with a carnival, musical performances, dinners—it is awesome. Each year, on Sunday morning, each of the three churches in town forfeit their normal Sunday services and come together in the park for a community-wide worship service. This year, I was contacted to see if I would be interested in providing the message for this particular service.

I was honored and excited to be able to do this. I thought it would be good for me personally, as well as my family and friends. The timing was important as the service would be held the day before what would have been…no, what was…Grayden's third birthday. This capped off a rough period that saw us dealing with several firsts: Jamie's birthday, father's day and Grayden's birthday in 16 days.

The service started with two songs, Tenth Avenue North's "Worn" and Addison Road's "What Do I Know of Holy?" and transitioned into the following:

"I have always found music to be healing—it speaks to me and allows me to experience things my own self-defenses keep from me. Music has become a part of me…so to those of you who know me, it is probably not a surprise to you that we begin our service this morning with two songs.

These particular songs tell two different stories to me. The first, is an illustration of how many of my days currently look and feel. Sometimes it is difficult to get out of bed. Sometimes it is difficult to stay out of bed. We don't yet have good days, we have what I call bad days and better days…and although we have experienced good moments, our hurt and sorrow still seems to trump many things.

The second song is a "hit the nail on the head" view of spirituality in my world. My entire life I have listened but have not effortlessly understood. I ask questions and don't trust the answers because I fear my own wants and needs, my own selfishness will trump what God is trying to teach me and/or tell me. It is my hunger to understand that keeps my focus where I want it to be.

Many of you know my family's story. And for those of you who do not, I am going to spend some time this morning telling you about our lives over the course of the past six months. In addition, I will be using some information presented to our congregation by our pastor, Jeremy Irwin in a recent message on grief…it spoke to me and I think there is information there that you might benefit from as well.

Today, we are going to take some time talking about and looking at grief. It is not a popular topic of conversation, but one that I believe resonates in every person here in some manner. Everyone knows it…society tends to marginalize some and heighten others…but loss is not something that is easy and it is not something that we are supposed to be good at. As we do this together this morning, the following things will probably happen:

1) I will do my best to give you a biblical perspective to which you will be able to understand and rely upon

2) We will talk about how impossible it is to "say the right things"

3) You will most likely see me cry…if you have not already…please forgive me in advance for any long and awkward pauses. If you become irritated and annoyed that I seem to be reading from a paper, please recognize that to some extent, that is by design. I am afraid making any eye contact might not be a good thing for my emotional strength and stability.

It is my hope that I can provide you with a sense of hope in and amongst your own grief…and I hope God will teach us all how to worship Jesus in our own pain.

The reason I want to tell you the particulars of this story is not to uphold us as a standard of virtue (this is what it means to suffer well). Jesus is our standard of virtue. Nor do I want you to think that your suffering is going to or should look exactly like ours does. However, I think naming things normalizes them. It creates an environment where people can talk about their own stories (things they did well, things they did poorly, when God seemed present, when God seemed absent, when they were full of inexplicable faith, when they were in the pit of despair). I also think giving you particulars, even if it's not the same as your suffering, is helpful.

So here's our story…Our lives changed Monday, January 28th at about 3:30 in the afternoon. I was home that day with the flu. Our babysitter Hannah was with the boys and, aside from me being under the weather, it was a normal Monday.

Hannah left at 3:00 and let me know the boys had a good day and told me Grayden had been asleep for almost three hours…which was not a surprise to me as he'd had a restless night of sleep. I assumed he was getting sick. At about 3:30, I decided it was probably time for Grayden to wake up. When I walked into his room, I saw our little guy lying peacefully on his stomach. I spoke to him and he did not stir. I placed my hand on his back and he did not respond. As I said his name, I rolled his body over and immediately knew what had happened. And even though I knew what had happened, I couldn't just stand there and not try to do something.

I grabbed him and screamed, yelling for Jamie to call 9-1-1. She was calm at the time and told me to start CPR. As I gave rescue breaths, I could smell and taste vomit on his lips…which was puzzling to me because there were no markings of such on his bed sheets. As his chest would decompress, I could hear a gurgling sound and I knew his lungs were filled with fluid…I was faced with our reality: Grayden went down for his nap a healthy, little boy full of potential and woke up in the arms of Jesus.

Our normal was destroyed and our lives were changed forever.

Those of you who met Grayden knew there was something special about him…
and of course, I am biased because I am his daddy…but I don't think anyone
who knows him will allow you to think any differently. He seemed to have that
"it" factor that made you want to be closer to him.

I want to share with you the eulogy we wrote for Grayden's services. I think it
is important to read this with you because a large part of dealing with grief is
facing those things that are difficult for us emotionally…and because I want
each of us to recognize that there is no shame in remembering those people
we love.

*It was truly our honor to get to be Grayden's mommy and daddy. From the moment
we found out he would be joining our family, we loved him without hesitation.*

*We prayed for him for over a year before we learned he would be blessing our lives…
and he never stopped doing that from that moment on.*

*If you never had the chance to spend any extended amount of time with him, please
let us show you who our boy is through our eyes…*

*Grayden seemed to have the ability to light up a room when he entered. His smile
was contagious and his dimples were simply too pronounced and perfect to overlook.
He often carried himself with a sheepish grin, an ornery smile or eyes that could tell
an entire story…and always, without a shadow of a doubt, his wrinkly eyebrows
would be present to welcome you. Grayden seemed to have a magnetic ability to
attract the attention of anyone who was close to him. He gave great hugs, was an
exceptional zerbert-giver and could stop even the hardest of souls in their tracks
with one single, "I love you."*

*Now, I know we are obviously biased, but Grayden was a pretty sharp young
man. He counted past 20 and knew all of his shapes—with his favorite being the
hexagon. We learned this when he requested his grilled cheese be cut into this…it
seems the option of two rectangles, three triangles and four squares were simply not*

good enough. He also was as bilingual as a two year-old from a single language family in the Midwest could get. Once when asked how many cars he had, he responded by saying "TRES"...not sure it would've been believable had he not held up three cars to prove his point. And we would be remised if we did not mention his clever ability prolong the bedtime routine. A personal favorite had to be when he was heard yelling, "Daddy, I need you to come in to my room...pleeeeeease daddy...I don't have any pants on.....I mean it, daddy, come in right now, Swiper the Fox swiped them!"

Grayden seemed to function at a level far ahead of his years. He quoted his first movie at the age of two. We heard him yelling from the bathtub he shared with his little brother... "Daddy, I touched the butt, I touched the butt" Daddy, being a bit confused came into the bathroom to see him holding up his toy boat...and then he explained, "I touched the butt, daddy...just like Nemo."

He was focused on doing everything fast. He wanted to run fast, to kick fast and to spin fast. (I have no idea where he learned to be competitive?!?)

He talked of his grandparents often and got excited every time there was a chance to talk to Grandma and Grandpa in Illinois. He loved Grandpa's train and always was ready for a ride on the big tractor. He loved to read books with Grandma, too. Grandma always played on the floor with him and they had a specific bedtime routine, complete with buttons and school bus books.

Grayden's Koko and Papa were two of his favorites as well. Grayden cooked with Koko and never missed an opportunity to rock with her. And unfortunately with our current string of unfortunate circumstances, Papa became "Mr. Fix-It." Anytime anything wasn't working, he would quickly say, "Papa fix it."

Grayden loved his little brother, Jayce. They played together every day...and Grayden, even though he got in a few legitimate shots, adored him. We constantly found ourselves saying, "Grayden, do not hug Jayce around the neck" and "Stop touching his face."

Grayden had many, many cousins that adored him as well...and he loved them all right back. He got so excited to see them that one time he even ran circles around the living room yelling, "thank you, thank you, thank you!"

We did everything we could to introduce him to Jesus. We talked about God openly, took Grayden to church on a regular basis and tried to explain why we pray and what purpose it served in our lives. Grayden became a serene little boy every time he heard us say, "It's time to say thank you to Jesus." He would stop what he was doing, fold his hands and prepare to listen.

Our favorite times were when we asked Grayden if he wanted to pray, and he said yes. His most memorable prayer went something like this: "Dear Jesus, um...I'm sorry I hit Jayce, um...and thank you for this food, Amen" And every time, without fail, Grayden would clap his hands and demand every person in the room do the same.

Our boy loved to be outside...and he played hard. Many times he would come back inside and his cheeks were flushed and his hair was damp with sweat...and he battled coming in, even though it was nearly dark and he could barely see.

Grayden had a soft spot for his shows: Dora, The Teenage Mutant "Engine" Turtles, Bob the Builder, Thomas the Train, Bubbleguppies, Elmo's World and Team "Zoomizoomi." He was growing a fondness for Disney movies and loved Mickey Mouse.

Grayden got to spend three days a week with Miss Hannah...and we feel so fortunate he was able to learn how much she loved him while he was with us. Having Hannah in our home allowed for our boys to have some amazing advantages and we are truly grateful for her presence in our lives.

We loved hugging Grayden because he was truly good at it. Best part about it was his hugs were often accompanied by a sincere and heartfelt question. Namely," "Are you happy, mommy?" and "Do I make you happy, Daddy?" We take so much joy from knowing that he understood these feelings. He knew we loved him because we verbalized it to him on a regular basis. We consistently asked him, "Who loves you?" and he would rattle off a list of at least 8 names—Mommy and Daddy and

Jayce were always first, and we adore that. And when we turned the tables and asked him who he loved, he always started his list by saying some combination of the same three names.

Our hearts are broken at the earthly loss of our young hero. And under normal circumstances, this formalized "goodbye" would be something that we could not comprehend. Instead, we choose to alter the words just a bit. Our goodbye, becomes, "we cannot wait to join you in heaven, our sweet and precious boy."

Mommy and daddy love you very much but we know that we took advantage of our opportunity to tell you about Jesus. Now, Grayden, heaven's newest and handsomest little man , it is Jesus' turn to tell you about us. We know you will enjoy learning up there as much as you did here.

We offer you to God with absolutely no regrets because mommy loved you "to pieces, to pieces, to pieces" and daddy consistently gave you "kisses, kisses, kisses, kisses, kisses."

Go now and be with Jesus and never hurt again. Be in your perfect, fever-free body and know that Mommy and Daddy will be along soon to join you."

That was who he was to us…and who he will always be in our eyes. We miss him so much, because we loved him that much.

Obviously, this particular day was the worst of my life…So I think it makes sense for people to wonder, for me to wonder, "Where was God on the worst day of my life?"

The truth is, most of us are not prepared to suffer and we are not prepared to be present with other people when they are suffering. In other words, we don't know how to suffer ourselves. We don't know how to suffer with others.

Why is that?

I think several arguments can be made here, but the best I can come up with is a simple idea--we're naïve. We don't really listen to God's Word--which tells us repeatedly that we are going to suffer. It is something we are going to encounter and we've got to be prepared, theologically and personally.

I would venture to guess that most of us actually believe more in karma than that the Almighty God of the universe, in His mercy, sends difficulties our way. Instead we believe the lie – if I'm good and if I do what God wants me to do... He owes me a pain-free life. Now, if that's your view... here's how you know... when bad things happen, you feel betrayed and victimized. And you say in your heart what Job's wife said in her suffering, "Let's curse God and die!" So we need the Bible, not our culture, to help us think about suffering.

The Bible says that God governs all things, including suffering. That the past, present, and future are His. That God has a purpose behind every ounce of our pain. It's not random, it's planned. And that Jesus uses suffering, in mysterious ways, never to punish us, but to refine us for our good and His glory. That's a Biblical view of suffering. Now, that's a lot, and we need to unpack it. But my point is this...

God wants to teach us how to honestly face suffering with courage and hope because of Jesus.

For those of you that have suffered, you know that you have to work through certain problems that it causes in your relationship with God.

You have to work through the intellectual problem – How can suffering exist if God is all-knowing, all-powerful and good?

But you also have to work through the personal problem – How can I keep trusting you Jesus when you could've changed this but didn't? Where is your wise, powerful goodness to me?

So I want to deal with the intellectual problem of suffering though a logical argument. And I want to deal with the personal problem through my own story of suffering and God's story of suffering.

The intellectual problem of suffering and evil…this is many people's main objection to Christianity.

Here's the argument:

"Suffering and evil exist."

"Therefore, an all-powerful, all-knowing, and good God does not exist."

At first glance, that seems like a slam dunk. But lets think a little deeper.

It is important to point out that it is not enough to simply make a claim; we have to explain why that claim is true.

Jay Sklar, a professor and author, gives this similar example - consider these two statements:

"All single men are bachelors."

"Therefore, John is not a bachelor."

True statement with a conclusion. But by themselves these are not an argument; the first statement does not necessarily lead to the second statement. In order for this to be an argument we need another statement in the middle. A bridge. Namely, "John is not a single man". Putting all three together gives us an argument:

"All single men are bachelors;

John is not a single man;

Therefore, John is not a bachelor."

In the same way, if we say that "suffering and evil exist" and "Therefore, an all-powerful, all-knowing, and good God does not exist", we have not made an argument. The first statement does not necessarily lead to the second statement. We need other statements in between. We need bridges.

Now, what might those bridges be? I would suggest they are as follows:

"Suffering and evil exist."

"An all-powerful, all-knowing, and good God would not permit evil unless there was a justifiable reason;"

"If there were a justifiable reason, it would be apparent to us what it was;"

"There does not appear to us to be any justifiable reason for evil;"

"Therefore, an all-powerful, all-knowing, and good God does not exist."

Now we have an argument. The argument only works, of course, if we know that each of these additional statements is true. If all of the premises are true, then the conclusion is true and the Bible is wrong. So, take a look. Is each additional statement here something that is necessarily true?

Many philosophers have pointed out that there is a huge assumption being made here in line 3 and 4. Namely, God may have reasons for allowing evil that we cannot even begin to imagine. One philosopher Alston, gets at this through some analogies.

Suppose I look at a painting by Picasso and say, "I cannot see any reason that would lead Picasso to arrange the figures in this painting the way he has, and because I cannot see the reason, he must not have one." You would say, "But Brent (Jeremy), Picasso is so far beyond you in terms of his knowledge of art, he may have reasons you can't even begin to imagine, and you should not assume that his reasons would be apparent to you."

Or again, if I listen to a Nobel-prize winning scientist state a new theory about quantum phenomena, and I say, "I cannot see any reason why she would come up with that theory, and because I cannot see the reasons, she must not have one," you would say, "But Brent, she is so far beyond you in terms of her knowledge of science, she may have reasons you cannot even begin to imagine, and you should not assume her reasons would be apparent to you."

In the same way, if I say, "I cannot see any reason why an all-powerful, all-knowing and good God would permit evil, and because I cannot see a reason, he must not have had one," then the proper response is, "But Brent, God is so far beyond you in terms of knowledge in general, he may have reasons you cannot even begin to imagine, and you should not assume his reasons would be apparent to you."

So... for those of you that are skeptical about the claims of Christianity, but also for all of us believers, it is crucial that we name this mystery of suffering. The Bible tells us that God has good reasons for allowing suffering in our lives, but very often those reasons are not explained to us. Sometimes in retrospect, we can appreciate some of the reasons. Many of us can point to very difficult seasons of life in which we grew and were shaped in ways that could have only have been produced by suffering. Nevertheless, the Bible does not give us a complete answer to the question, "Why?" And yet, our suffering does not mean He's not good or He didn't know about it or He's powerless to do anything about it.

It means that God's goodness is sometimes very mysterious. His brilliant, loving, master plan includes things we would never include. Though He is never responsible for evil, He allows and uses it in our lives, for our good.

That's logical, but it's hardly satisfying, right?

And it leads us straight to the personal problem of suffering – How can I keep trusting/loving a God who could've changed this but didn't? Jesus, where is your powerful, wise, goodness to me? Where were you on the worst day of my life?

Suffering feels like having a blanket between you and the world. Very alienated.

Everyone else's life keeps going and yours stops.

Life slows down. You don't think about 5 and 10 year plans, you think, "can I handle this afternoon?" You are in survive mode...not in thrive mode. Your goals change from making something happen to making it through the day.

Your views change. You stop assuming certain things are going to happen in a linear, easy fashion.

You gain a sense of the fragility and brokenness of the world. Things are not the way they're supposed to be. You see it everywhere in ways that you overlooked before.

Revisit some of your assumptions about God and realize that He hasn't promised certain things that we might have assumed He has promised. God never promises children or spouses or long life or health. Not even to righteous people. Luke 1 – Elizabeth and Zechariah were blameless and barren. That's possible...in fact, common.

We discovered that you don't just grieve once. Random things set off sad and angry memories. It creeps up when you're not looking for it...you exhale and there it is--fresh wave of grief. Other times you just feel numb. That's okay. Or even guilty that you're not more sad than you are. We learned not to judge our grief, but to name it and share it.

For those of you that think being a Christian means always being happy, or pretending things don't hurt... that grief is somehow un-Christian, I remind you "If he was worth loving, he is worth grieving" and grief is an expression of love.

Managing this pain, however, became unbearable in our situation...we found ourselves having to manage people's responses because they were uncomfortable around us and could not find a way to find comfort...we took on the task of managing other people's pain as well because they felt an intense desire to grieve for us and with us...and we somehow felt responsible for their pain and grief.

Simply put, nobody knows what to say. And... it became exhausting.

Many people have asked us what they should've said, how they should've responded and how they can best care for people in our situation in the future.

Again, I reiterate, there is nothing that can be said that stops the pain…and in the midst of it all, that is what we wanted more than anything else. We wanted him back…that was the only fix…and it was an impossibility.

The closest thing we heard to being spot on was from the best man in our wedding. He said he went into his pastor's office and shut the door, sat down in front of him and said, "What can I tell them that will make this better… you've got to give me something that I can say to them that will not make this seem so awful."

He told me his pastor reclined in his office chair, put his hands above his head, signed and said, perhaps the most profound thing in the history of the world, "You tell them this…this is crappy."

The entire situation is a duel-edged sword because there truly was nothing anyone could say that would make the situation better. It's a hard position to be in as a friend or loved one. You have to feel out what people want and you need to know, you're probably going to screw it up. That's okay. Please, please, please recognize that there really is nothing to say…and recognize also that we, the grievers, are aware of this. Those grieving do not look to you to fix anything—remember, it cannot be fixed…they look to you for support and comfort.

So if you find yourself saying, "There really are no words…trust that and don't spend the next 5-10 minutes trying to struggle upon something profound and brilliant."

I want each of you to know that we recognize and adore the effort…and we do not judge you or hold your attempts against you. We see them for exactly what they are…a loving outreach from someone who loves us. My advice to you is this…just love them and don't feel like you have to speak. Hug them, be available to them and offer support…then re-offer it 2 months after things settle down for everyone else. Normal does not re-establish itself following the loss of a family member that quickly…those grieving will still be hurting then.

More specifically, I would recommend you avoid the saying the following things in the initial midst of loss:

"God is teaching you through this." Yes, but that doesn't make the pain go away, nor does it provide a full explanation. I doubt God, who loves me, would have put me through all this in order to make me a marginally better comforter"… and that is okay.

"I understand what you are going through…I lost my son, or my grandmother or my cat (I actually heard this at another funeral we attended from an individual I'd never met before)…regardless how similar the parallels are (and to be honest, some we heard were not remotely similar), no one understands what that person is feeling. And that is okay…that person does not feel guilt because you do not understand it…he does not wish it upon you either…And that is okay.

"He is in a better place now" I know exactly where he is…and I love it and hate it at the same time—and that is confusing to me…but the truth is , in that moment, hate and pain trump everything else. There is no immediate comfort in the idea that he is in heaven…because right after you lose him, the only thing you want is for him to be with you again…and that, is okay.

"Your little boy is an angel now" Let's be honest, he is not. God made angels as individual beings. Human begins are not transformed into angel status upon entry to heaven. I thoroughly believe Grayden is hanging out with the Angels, but do not believe he is one…and that is okay.

"Stay Strong" I hate this one the most. Mostly because I don't want to be strong… and probably because I do not define strength the same way society does. I don't want to be strong, I want to be weak…in fact, the Bible tells us to be weak and draw our strength from Him. Perhaps take care of yourself and your family is a better way to say that…that's the basis of the message anyway, right?

The Bible says that we have to bear each other's burdens. So, if people close to you are suffering, I would say this - Don't ignore it (it's the elephant in the room). Ignoring will make them feel like you don't care. But don't push it. Pushing it will make it feel like you're entitled or you're trying to fix it.

Ask them if they want to talk about it. Ask them to tell their story and just listen. Don't fix. Don't judge. Ask them how they are feeling, but give them an out (you don't have to say anything if you don't want to). Tell them that you're sorry. That's good to hear and you can't say much more than that. Tell them that you're praying for them. That's good, too.

Good comforters learn to listen to people.

You learn to ask good questions to people that are suffering. Not to wrap it up into a neat little box. But to draw them out and let them talk honestly (if they want to).

You also learn that it's a privilege when people let you into their pain. It's not your right. You don't deserve to know. It's a true honor when they share their hurt with you. Don't trample on it. Don't belittle it. Listen. Pray.

Jesus wept and taught us to "weep with those who weep." The best thing that Job's friends did when they saw his misery is they sat with him for 7 days in silence.

Your presence is healing whether you say anything or not.

What else is helpful?

- Cards and phone calls are nice...they are subtle pick me ups.
- We had members of our bible study scheduled to come three days a week...one to clean, one to grocery shop and one for laundry.
- Our church prepared a meal calendar for us.
- It was important to us...or at least to me, to memorialize him... because not only was he worth loving and grieving, he is also worth remembering. We collected money for a playground to be built at our church—and I will love watching kids play there because of him...and

we also created a memorial garden in front of our house in his honor—filled it with bright colors, things that remind us of him and flowers that attract butterflies and hummingbirds. Supporting a memorial is a way to illustrate that someone matters. I didn't understand this until Grayden died.

- We randomly receive packages in the mail with a note that says something to the effect of, "wanted Grayden to have this for his garden." I cannot tell you how cool it is to get those notes and to know that, not only is someone thinking about us…but about him, too.

- I get random messages just checking in on me.

- We are flooded with notes on our birthdays and on mother's and father's days…we recognize that and it helps.

All of these are subtle attempts to try to make things okay. But death is not okay. At the end of the story, Jesus doesn't make peace with death, he conquers it. So it won't help us to try to disown our pain. Rather, we have to take it to God…who legitimately understands grief and loss.

Consider the cross from the perspective of God:

God lost a son…he killed his son. His Son volunteered to be killed by God so that he could save his many others sons and daughters.

The heart of God must be struggling…he is pouring his furious wrath on His beloved, he's cutting off the one who was part of Himself.

In processing the anguish of heaven because of the death of the Son…God weeps and the angels are horrified.

That the Father would exclude and kill his Son so that instead of excluding and killing us, He might shower us with His love and approval forever should be humbling.

I knew our child for two and a half years and I was heart-broken at his death. Our Father had known his Son for eternity. Can you imagine his anguish? And yet something deeper than His anguish… his commitment to love us meant that he had to see his son's death through…and he did it.

Which brings us back to our question: how can a good, all-powerful, all-knowing God allow suffering and evil? We simply do not know what the answer is, but we do know what the answer is not: it is not because he doesn't care; it is not because he doesn't love us; it is not because he doesn't understand.

Look at the cross where Jesus suffered for us.

See, Jesus doesn't give us an answer to our suffering, instead He shares it. He suffered alongside of us, but even more, He suffered in our place. He took the suffering that we deserved. Because He was cut off from the Beloved Father. And we, who deserved to be cut off… are now brought close, embraced and are eternally loved by God.

So, Christ comforts us in our pain. He knows what it's like. So you can talk to Him about your pain. And He understands. He sympathizes. He helps and heals.

And that is how we can face suffering with courage and hope.

Because we have a suffering Savior who loves us. Because Jesus is with us. And this same Jesus has promised that He is coming back to wipe every tear away from our eyes. And to make all things new.

So, somehow, He is going to take even our current sorrow and use it in such a way that it enhances our joy in heaven. Imagine that you have a nightmare in which your loved ones die… and then you wake up and find they are alive and well. What do you do? You love them and appreciate them more than ever. Your night-marish sorrow enhances your joy. That's what God is going to do with our sorrow when He makes all things new.

Not only does Jesus share our pain, and comfort us in our pain, He redeems our pain. Your suffering is not in vain.

That is His plan for us.

Jesus uses our sorrow for His glory and for our good.

So… let me challenge you with the following:

1. Bring your suffering to Jesus. He loves you and gave Himself up for you.

2. Share your story. Let others into your pain.

3. If you are avoiding others who are hurting, apologize to them for your negligence, and "join them on the bench of mourning," so you can be a tangible expression of Christ's love to them.

I invite you to praise God even when things are unbearable…praise Him through your storm. Do this because of the promise He made to you…that you, even though you might feel small and unworthy of many things, are always worthy and even entitled to God's love. Regardless of who you see yourself to be, God loves you.

If you find death to be a particular struggle…or if life, in general is a struggle and you can not make sense of how to deal with what might feel completely overwhelming and encompassing, look to God for comfort.

Since Grayden died, I have been more focused on heaven than ever before. It was always something that peaked my interest…but in the past it was always a little scary to me…not heaven itself, but the idea that I might not make it in.

I used to think that if my good outweighed my bad, that heaven would be my reward…that if I was mostly successful obeying the ten commandments, that I would get to experience heaven—I mean seriously, if I am good on 7 or 8 of the 10, that should be enough, right? I subscribed to this checklist idea of how admittance to heaven worked.

What I found out along the way, long before we lost Grayden is that God's checklist did not look anything like my own. What God is seeking is his inclusion in our lives.

If you want to experience heaven, make the choice.

If you are unsure what that means…allow me to present the following illustration that may or may not make sense to you:

"Dear God, I am struggling, I am hurting and there are times, even when I am surrounded by large numbers of family and friends, that I feel alone. I am confused and I want things to make sense…the only problem is, I can't seem to find anything that will clarify my confusion…and believe me, I have tried to find this on my own. So…I turn to you.

I ask you to come into my heart and stay there. I want you to be my savior and I want that to become a regular part of my day. I recognize I am a sinner and will make changes in the way I do things…even those that will be difficult, God.

I will make changes in my life and seek to live in the manner you want me to. I give myself to you, and in turn, ask you to live in me."

When I did that…and as I continue to make that the guideline by which I live my life, I got my ticket to heaven. It is my responsibility to see it through…and I am hungry to experience heaven. I cannot wait to be there…to experience everything…to take it all in…and I want you to be there with me.

John 5:24 reads, "Very truly I tell you, whoever hears my word and believes Him who sent me has eternal life and will not be judged but has crossed over from death to life."

I hope that in some way, God spoke to you this morning. And I invite you to explore the possibilities. Each day we are given an endless amount of possibilities. God provides us the fuel to light our fires. It is our responsibility to make sure we allow people to see the light.

If there are things going on in your head that you do not clearly understand and you need to process through this, I invite you to come forward after the service. I will get you connected to someone who can listen and can offer you support. Pastors from community congregations, if you are able and willing, and wouldn't mind wandering up to the front following our benediction, I would appreciate it. If there are people who request specific prayer, I would like to get them connected with someone locally.

We are going to end this morning's services with an atypical benediction. I invite you to sit back, soak up a beautiful melody and take in a powerful message through music.

"Go Light Your World" By Chris RIce

"God is good and we are fortunate to know that. Thank you for spending a part of your morning with us. I hope each of you find God's blessing as you start the rest of you day…go in peace."

Changed the name of my fantasy football team

Hurricane Ditka was my go-to fantasy name. It was a play off a Saturday Night Live skit with Chris Farley and George Wendt. It was the perfect way to pay homage to both Coach Ditka and Farley—two of my favorites.

But this particular year, I needed something different.

After playing around with several alternatives like "Steele's Magnolias," "Black and Blue and Grayden," and "Men of Steele," I decided on "Grayden Steele Curtain."

It might seem simple, but working him into something I enjoyed was therapeutic. It was a safe and creative way to remember him.

My fantasy teams were terrible, but I had the best name in each of the leagues I was in.

Bought family Teenage Mutant Engine Turtle pajamas for Christmas

When we talked about Christmas traditions, and what we would do with our family, it was important to me that we adopt a couple of things from my family.

First, we got an ornament every year. Not only was it something I looked forward to every year, but when we "grew up" and had our first tree, it would be full of personal ornaments and not be thrown together at the last minute. I loved this idea and looking for the perfect ornament for each member of my family has become one of my favorite parts of holiday shopping.

Second, we always got a game every year. I used to joke that family game night was invented at my house…and that was why I wanted to use this particular tradition for my family as well. I want to be an active family that does things together and having games to play promotes that. I love the interaction that comes from playing games…I love the teachable moments, I love the friendly competition and I love the time together.

Jamie has great memories from family Christmases but didn't really have any specific traditions that she wanted to continue. So, when she said she wanted us to do Christmas pajamas every year, I thought it was a great idea.

Jamie would buy mine, I would buy hers and we would buy pajamas for the kids together. We would wear them Christmas morning and every year, with any luck, it would be something we would all look forward to.

This year, we chose Teenage Mutant "Engine" Turtle pajamas.

It was a tribute to our boy and was highlighted by the fact that, out of the blue, Jayce began to refer to them the same way. Grayden was the first person I ever heard refer them as Engine Turtles…and Jayce was the second.

We rocked out the "Engine Turtle" family pajamas this year!

Thankfully for us, there were multiple choices for turtle pajamas this year. I love the picture of us all wearing our matching pajamas. And even though Jayce will hate them in 10 years, I cannot wait to see what we come up with next. We will take a picture, for sure.

Let his brother pick out a Halloween costume

Some people probably consider me cheap. I would call it frugal and/or financially responsible, but don't have a problem with cheap.

There are certain things I try to save money on. For instance, we have learned that if we shop after the holidays, we can save a ton of money if we buy things once they have been drastically discounted. We keep a gift closet upstairs for Christmas and birthday gifts—it just makes sense.

Likewise, Halloween costumes get marked down anywhere from 50%-90% after the season, too. I have always been the guy who would buy two or three costumes when they are marked down and guestimate what the boys would want to wear the following Halloween and then do my best to talk them into it.

When we lost Grayden, this changed. All of a sudden, spending $20 on a Halloween costume didn't even phase me.

When I thought about Grayden's last Halloween, I realized he never got to pick out his costume and I decided that Jayce, as soon as he was old enough to have an opinion, would not have that issue.

I took Jayce to the store right after the new costumes hit the rack. I secretly hoped he would pick Spider-Man because we'd planned to have a Spider-Man themed costume party for his birthday on the 25th. I found some Spider-Man plates and napkins marked down and thought it would work out nicely. Realistically, I knew this probably wouldn't happen, but I was still hopeful.

As we walked down the aisle, we found Superman, Batman, Spider-Man, Captain America and Thomas the Train…I was sure he would pick Thomas the Train…but thankfully, I was wrong.

Without any encouragement from me, Jayce reached for the Spider-Man costume and said, "I want Spider-Man, daddy"

And Spider-Man it was.

He wore that costume at least a dozen times before Halloween, and he's worn it at least that many times since. Maybe I would've figured this out eventually anyway. But for now, our days of re-using hand-me-down costumes are over.

Grayden went trick-or treating once and he loved it. Seeing his response that night is something that will never leave me. And because of that, I will treat Halloween a little bit differently from now on.

It is as simple as this, Grayden's death has taught me to not take anything for granted…to seize opportunities and to not miss an opportunity because I make finances, or anything else, more important than memories.

Spider-Jayce at
Halloween 2013

Experienced Christmas morning without him

Jayce at Christmas 2013

We were able to find joy in the moment, but not without some sadness. Our incomplete family was trying to celebrate a morning that had always been about family to me. How did we do that missing one of our own?

We smiled and were excited for Jayce…and it was not an artificial excitement. We were thrilled to be sharing the experience with him. We just missed his big brother.

At the end of that particular day, we smiled more than we cried—and I am calling that a victory. It was another horrid first we could cross off the list.

We expected it to be difficult and it was.

Our biggest victory that day was being able to find joy amongst our immense and overpowering pain. How did we do that?

We talked about him, we shared gifts that paid tribute to him and we loved each other.

We opened stockings, and talked about the things we did we did when we were kids. We hung our new ornaments on the tree and laughed at our favorite lines from our favorite Christmas movies. We talked to Jayce about the gift of Christ's birth and told him about what Christmas is really about.

By not ignoring our pain, we gave ourselves a chance. There is no reasonable way that we make it through that day without thinking about him. So with that in mind, it would be silly to try.

I have found that embracing our reality, and facing the negatives head on, was a good thing for us. Going through the motions only prolongs the inevitable. We realized that at about the six-month mark.

Christmas was the last big thing we'd have to experience for the first time without him. So we embraced it. We allowed ourselves to feel. We laughed, we cried and we loved. All things considered, it was a good day.

Got confirmation from his brother that sub two year olds listen and comprehend

My conversation with an 18 month old Jayce:

Me: Do you love Daddy?

Jayce: Yes

Me: Does daddy love you?

Jayce: Yes

Me: Do you love mommy?

Jayce: Mommy...yes

Me: Does mommy love you?

Jayce: yes

Me: Do you love Grayden? ...Do you remember your brother?

Jayce: He's in heaven

Me: (instant tears)

Jayce: (touching my face...) Crying...kisses, daddy

For those of you who've asked if Jayce gets it, I think he does!

Figured out how to change his room without eliminating his memory

Grayden's first room, was no longer his room.

Shortly after he died, we made the decision to move Jayce in there. It made the most sense and we thought it would be good to not be afraid to go in there.

I struggled with the idea of painting over his name. I'd painted it on the wall when he was a baby.

There was a part of me that wanted to leave it...and a part of me that thought it would be best to paint over it. I was lost in what was right and I was stuck in what to do next.

I talked about it. I talked about it to anyone who would listen. It was one of the first things I worried about right after we lost him. I needed to lead my family and I had no clue how to do that. His name on the wall represented our past and present. And all of a sudden, his future was taken from us. Did painting over that embrace that truth? Was it just a necessary next step?

We wanted that room to be Jayce's. He deserved that.

At our weekend retreat, I asked how others in our situation had dealt with room changes and similar tough decisions.

I remember learning that there was no right answer…and that was disappointing. If only there was a manual, then things would be so much easier.

Ultimately, we realized that if he were still with us, his room would go through changes. That realization helped us be okay with switching things up.

My wife had the brilliant idea to make subtle changes.

By painting over the "G", "R" and "N", and painting over the staff of the "D", we would only need to add the "J" to spell Jayce's name.

We left the original letters in green, and would add the enhanced "C" and new "J" in blue. This would spell JayCe but would still include GRayDeN.

I loved it…and I think about both my boys every time I look at it.

Worried about how to make sure he was a presence in our home without it becoming a shrine to him

Super Grayden strutting in Katie's shades

I had been in houses that had a 5X7 frame of a deceased loved one at every turn. I found no fault in them doing that, but did not want that for us.

When I see that, it seems to be an illustration of pain. And while I wanted our house to be a place we saw him, I didn't want it to be a shrine to him.

Over the course of the year, we figured out how to do this. We made conscious decisions about how he would be represented in our home.

We decided his baby picture will always hang over our fireplace—right next to his brother's. The collage frame of his first photo shoot will always have a place in our home...and it will most likely hang right next to his brother's.

As our family grows and ages, change will come. We are committed to changing our home with it.

He is represented in the same amount of pictures as his brother. He will be represented in a parallel fashion to any other future siblings he might have as well. The only difference will be, our pictures of him will never be any different than they are now. But that does not diminish his place in our family and how he will be represented in our home.

He appears as a part of our family...and that is important to us, because he is a part of our family.

I suspect this will always be a work in progress...constantly something we will be cognizant of.

Our little Superman will always be represented in our home...but he will never be over-represented and we will do everything we can to make sure it never feels like he is a more important than anyone else.

Worked hard to make sure his brother did not experience a different upbringing because of his loss

I want Jayce to have a normal childhood. I want to be a good father and I want him to look back as an adult and have positive things to say about his childhood.

I believe I am a good father. I work hard to be consistent and do my best to be a role model and teacher to my boys. I want them to be well-behaved but have personality. I want them to be a bit ornery but know the difference between right and wrong.

We were on our way…and then Grayden died.

I was so concerned that after this happened, I would be too lenient. Then I was concerned that because I was concerned about being too lenient, that I would over-compensate and be too hard on him.

It took me a while to realize that Grayden's death didn't have to have an effect on how I raised his brother. So I made the decision to be the same father I was…to be the same father I would've been if he were still here. If what I was doing was good enough before, there is no reason it should not be good enough now.

Grayden was trying to be sweet,
but Jayce wasn't having it

Held his brother
a bit more

I missed him.

I wanted to hold him, to feel his heartbeat, to know how he felt close to me.

The only problem was, I couldn't do that anymore.

I ached at his absence. I feared that something would happen to Jayce, too. Sometimes the anxiety consumed me. I struggled to sleep. I struggled to be comfortable in our home.

To combat this, I held Jayce a bit more…and there is nothing wrong with that.

Jayce was not a replacement for Grayden. He never could be. Instead, he was a reminder…not of his brother, but of life. I embraced that life wholeheartedly.

Maybe my favorite picture of them we have…
I love the pride in Grayden's eyes

Celebrated him on holidays

We went trick-or-treating approximately three months before he died. I will never forget that night.

We almost cancelled. I thank God we didn't. He had a ball that night. Once he figured out he would get candy at every house we went to, his little legs were consistently moving as fast as I'd ever seen them go. Candy was a treat—not something we kept around the house.

Had we not gone out that night, he would not have had a chance to experience trick-or-treating. That night he wore a monkey costume. He was a cute, little monkey.

When our first Halloween without him came, we did nothing different. (We did that on purpose.) It poured the evening we had set to go out to trick-or-treat. Jayce had a nagging cold so we made the executive decision to wait until next year. I hated it, but I knew it was the right call. We found other ways for Jayce to experience Halloween. It was a good holiday—even thought he was not with us.

We told our families we were pregnant with Grayden at Thanksgiving. I remember talking about being thankful for the blessing of our family growing. We'd struggled for over a year to get pregnant and were so excited he was on his way.

My dad's "thing" with the grandkids is calling them "turkeys." With that being said, Thanksgiving became more important to our family. We could celebrate the turkey, so to speak. We got dad an 8-foot inflatable Turkey and the kids love seeing it.

Grayden wore his turkey hat and consistently showed off how cute he was.

Our first Thanksgiving without him, I was thankful for salvation and heaven, which meant I would see him again.

Grayden's first Halloween

Pumpkin painting with Daddy at age 2

Grayden the turkey on his
first Thanksgiving

St. Patrick's Day –
2 years old

St. Patrick's Day was the day after my birthday. We spent it in Tennessee at our retreat. We were surrounded by couples who'd also lost a young child.

There was no green beer or Irish food.

His death was new to us at that point and we spent the entire weekend celebrating him, and the lives of 14 other little boys and girls. Even though it was extremely difficult, it was an inspiring weekend that was exactly what we needed.

He got to go Easter egg hunting. I am so thankful he did, too. His little legs were moving fast. Once he figured out the purpose, he was pretty efficient.

Grayden loved candy...and although he didn't get it often, Easter and Halloween were certainly times it was in the house.

One of my favorite Grayden stories involves a van full of people, Grayden in his car seat and a wrapper in a purse.

Our Aunt was rifling through her purse and took an old wrapper out. Grayden heard the rippling noise from the wrapper (and thinking it was a piece of candy) put his arm up in the air and said, "I'll have one, please."

Our last Christmas with him was a bittersweet one. Christmas the year before we lost him proved to be an important one.

We were not in a good place financially and made the decision that we would forego Christmas this particular year. Jamie and I were fine with utilizing our financial resources elsewhere and knew that our boys would be taken care of by our family and friends. We had ornaments for each of the boys and we made them a few gifts, but other than that, we'd decided to do that would be our best choice. We knew the boys would never remember and we were content with the decision.

When our neighbor randomly showed up with multiple armfuls of gifts, I did not know at the time what it would really mean to me.

For starters, it sincerely brought joy to our entire house. But the most important thing that act of kindness gave us was a lasting picture of Grayden experiencing Christmas in our home--in our living room, in front of our tree.

When we first experienced Christmas without him, I was concerned I couldn't do it. What I learned as it occurred, was that I just didn't want to do it. It seemed wrong to not have him with us. I didn't like it...not at all. But the idea that "I couldn't do it" was just not accurate.

So much of what we did that year involved trying to identify a "new normal" and attempting to find peace and joy in moving on without him. It was a difficult walk. Sometimes we handled it better than others.

Easter-Age 2

However, a year later, we are much better equipped to deal with the thought of moving on with our lives. To not do that would yield a sense of stagnancy that would eventually suffocate us.

We were looking at a couple of possibilities: live the rest of our lives in bitterness, sadness and disappointment...or, continue to seek contentment and happiness as we live as God wants us to.

When I think of it in that manner, there really isn't an argument. Executing that plan was a bit more difficult, but we were committed to doing so—and we were successful.

Peekaboo Santa Grayden rocking the Rudolph slippers

Watched my Dad struggle through Christmas

Asleep on the couch following a long day

Grandpa working on those leg muscles

Grayden loved his grandpa…he loved all of his grandparents. There really seemed to be a special connection with my dad, though.

Maybe it was because Grayden was the first grandchild that would pass on the family name? When he was born, there were no other Hickenbottom boys in Grayden's generation.

Maybe it was because Grayden was the first grandson born to one of dad's sons? Who knows?

My dad is the kind of guy people want to be noticed by. They wanted to be recognized by him and they wanted his approval. Dad has that "it" factor. I am not even sure what it is, but he has it. Call it charisma, charm or a mix of those things, but as a lifelong educator, he would have 20 people stand up and say something amazing about him for every one who would complain (and that number might be low.)

When Dad talked about Grayden, as with all of his grandkids, he lit up. He was proud of him, and if you asked dad, Grayden might have been the most advanced two year old in the history of the world. While that is certainly a biased assessment, I cannot help but think that dad saw that special something in Grayden that so many others see in him.

When Grayden died, my dad was angry. He was heartbroken, confused and disappointed. The thing I remember most, though, is the anger.

He stomped his feet repeatedly as he paced and would mutter or yell, "Why couldn't it have been me," "It doesn't make any sense," and "It's not fair."

Christmas proved to be particularly difficult for dad this year. To him, Christmas was about family. All dad cared about was that everyone got to be together…and this year, we were missing a part of our family.

We watched him tear up as we gave mom a figure of an angel walking with a little boy…and then again when she opened a figure of a grandma rocking a baby.

When dad gave Jayce his set of tractors, he struggled to find the words to say, "I had a hard time just buying one." He smiled as Jayce opened it and got excited…but you could tell he was missing Grayden.

My dad, as evidenced in the picture below, was proud of Grayden from the moment he first saw him…and will remain proud of him until the day he, too, goes to be with Jesus. I look forward to the day we can all go fishing and play catch together.

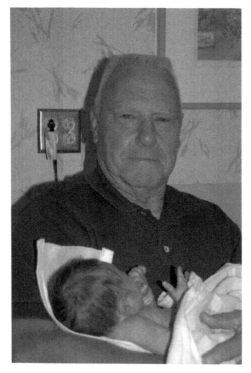

A proud grandpa meeting
Grayden for the first time

Struggled to feel and wondered what was wrong

A facebook post:

"Have felt kind of broken of late...forgot how to cry and can't seem to miss him like I think I should.

I cried tonight...and it was a good one. Never thought I'd say that was a relief... but I feel tremendously better.

He should be here and I cannot get over that...but it felt good to have a normal reaction tonight.

I have only been able to be emotional at church--and even that has been guarded...that is just not me.

I spent some time watching videos and remembering him as I couldn't sleep..I hate that he is not here--am still thrilled he is dancing with Jesus...just missing my boy."

I think it is important to realize there are going to be ups and downs: Times where you cannot feel and others when you cannot stop feeling. Instances when you are overwhelmed and others when you are numb.

As it turns out, I needed some time for things to regulate—and they did... until they didn't again.

After a while, I let go of the idea of control and decided to roll with the punches.

That is when things got easier.

Couldn't sleep when
I heard a noise

His death changed me.

I had to re-teach myself to remember that kids wake up from their naps. Well over 99% of children wake up from their naps every day. I mean, they just don't randomly die in their sleep for no apparent reason.

But Grayden did.

And now, because of this, my irrational fear of this happening to Jayce, consumed me from time to time.

I can hear some of your thinking, "but it is completely understandable, considering what happened," or "That makes complete sense." But the truth is, regardless of the circumstances, to worry obsessively about our healthy child not waking up from his sleep *IS* an irrational fear. And it is one that I have to deal with.

Our counselor told me I was suffering from Post Traumatic Stress Disorder (PTSD) about nine months into our grief counseling sessions. Even though I suspected this, there was both relief and shame in hearing him say that.

In my mind, PTSD was reserved for war heroes. Although, I understand the diagnoses, there was something about it being applied to me that seemed undeserved. It was as if I didn't want to take anything from people who "deserved it."

That is when I realized that there was neither pride nor shame involved with this particular label. In talking about it with Jamie, it became clear that like anyone else who deals with this, I didn't ask for, nor did I want to be experiencing it.

It affected me most at night. I missed him most when it was quiet. When Jamie and Jayce slept, everything was amplified.

Every noise made me jump. My heart raced and my protective instincts kicked in. It became a compulsion—I had to check on Jayce. I could not let the same thing happen to him that happened to Grayden. I knew it wasn't my fault, but at the same time, I wasn't able to prevent it, either.

When I realized my inability to not respond irrationally to sound was effecting Jayce's sleep, I knew I needed to make some changes. We purchased a video monitor and that helped. I limited the amount of times I would let myself go in his room to one. I remember what a relief it was when I first made it an entire night without opening his door to check on him.

And while things certainly got better, I was far from being comfortable with the noises. My responses ranged from raised heartbeat to what I would consider a panic attack.

The anti-anxiety meds seemed to help take the edge off, but I was still super reactive to sound when Jayce was sleeping. So much so that it affected my sleep as well.

My anxiety as far as Jayce is concerned is still a work in progress. I am learning to cope and am facing the issue head on. I would like to say it gets easier every day, but the truth is, it is a bit of a roller coaster.

I share this, not to bring attention to myself, but instead to highlight and illustrate a different response a parent experiences when losing a child. I will look at each similar situation I encounter in the future with a bit more compassion and empathy because of it.

Hated being inspirational, then learned to embrace it

It started shortly after he died.

People were constantly telling us how they admired us: our strength, our courage, our ability to find the silver lining, etc. It should've been uplifting and encouraging. Instead, because I was in such a horrible place, it was not. It was the opposite: suffocating, exhausting and filled with pressure.

Here's the thing—I knew I was going to fall apart. How disappointed would people be when that happened? I knew people were watching us, or at least observing us.

My real issue was with the pressure. It was pressure I put on myself, but it was pressure nonetheless. That is how I have always been—why put your name on something that you wouldn't want to do well? I saw these comments, at least for a short time, not as a sign of encouragement, but as an opportunity to fail.

I was selfish.

After a while, it was something I knew I had to deal with. So I went to the pastor from my church growing up. I respected him so much and I knew he would understand my question: "How do you respond to people saying you are inspiring? I know it should be a good thing...and it is...but all I feel is pressure."

His response was brilliant, like I knew it would be.

"You have to remember that it is okay that people watch you because that means they are looking for an opportunity to care for you. And most importantly, you have to remember that, as far as judgment goes, you only answer to God. No one expects you to be perfect, and if they do they have unrealistic expectations."

It was the correct answer, and exactly what I needed to hear.

I made some choices and they were beneficial. From that point on, I would do my best to accept the complements as such. I would not read more into them than was necessary and I would focus on the positive nature of the comment. I would use it to inspire and encourage myself...not as another component of stress in my life.

I let a good thing become a negative one, I take pride in the fact that I overcame that. After all, who doesn't want to be inspiring? Who doesn't want to make a difference? Who doesn't want to be a role model?

These were all the things I wanted for Grayden. I would be hypocritical if I didn't strive for those things in my own life.

My parents have been my
inspiration for years

Made a tie dyed
t-shirt with his brother

My students at Fontbonne University invited me to a tie-dye day in the "quad" area of their campus. They told me they'd had shirts made in Grayden's memory and they asked me if I could attend.

Luckily, it worked into my schedule and Jayce and I were able to take part.

The shirts were amazing.

His initials, along with the saying from his funeral service appeared in black as a heart patch on the front. When I first saw it, I got a little teary-eyed. I didn't even realize there was anything printed on the back until after Jayce and I had finished shirts for both me and Jamie.

Printed on the back were three, two-word sayings that I think sum up what I would've wanted for my boy.

Be Yourself

Have Fun

Love Life

It was the perfect message to mesh the life of a two and a half year old with something that would also speak to college students.

The results were fantastic. Jayce had a ball, and we have a keepsake we will never get rid of. I was so proud of them and grateful for what they did for him, and for our family.

Recognized social media
was a good thing for me

I spent a lot of time reading…as much as my eyes could handle. I found strength and peace in the words, understanding and encouragement of our friends and family.

Facebook was a good tool for this. It gave me something positive to focus on and I used it…repeatedly.

I read and re-read things. It was a distraction and a comfort. And perhaps most important of all, it was s safe outlet that let me react however I needed to privately.

I do not consider myself a private person, but what was happening all of a sudden changed that temporarily.

There was a lot of pressure to comfort others as they struggled and to be honest, that became burdensome at times. I wanted to support people who were struggling with this but it was difficult to manage the wide range of emotions Jamie, Jayce and I were experiencing—and that had to be my focus.

For as much gossip and junior high drama that social media can breed, in this instance, I am thankful for its existence.

Grayden's first ever "selfie"
with Miss Hannah

Made new friends

One of the joys that came from this experience are the new, amazing people that are now in our lives because of our boy.

We met eleven couples at Respite Retreat, our weekend retreat for couples who've lost a young child. We keep in touch on Facebook and I fully expect reunions and road trips with them.

Additionally, we have been connected with other people that had heard of what happened. People that we'd never met, contacted us and sent us cards of support. Jamie went to a retreat in St. Louis for mothers who'd lost children and developed some lasting friendships from that.

I wanted Grayden to grow up to be the kind of person that brought people together. I wanted him to be a "difference maker" and a role model.

Although he didn't get the opportunity to grow up here, with us, I found some comfort in the idea that he truly was a "game changer" and that he was successful in bringing people together.

When I think of him, I smile before I cry. I would've loved to see him grow, mature and develop. I looked forward to each of those things. Now, instead of looking forward, I look up—and to a different future, and eternal one.

Utilized Facebook to access my support system

This is what was on my mind in July…he would've turned three the month before…

six months ago today, our family was changed forever. We became incomplete--a little less loud and with a little less gusto. We miss him every day and lean on each other as we move on and learn our new normal.

Thank you for loving us…and for remembering him. As we continue to heal and move forward, he is still a part of us--even though his presence in our lives has been altered.

Missing my boy, loving my family and friends.

Prior to his death, I didn't often post on social networking sites. When I did it was to tell a story about our boys or to share something funny or ironic that we'd experienced.

This changed when we lost him.

I read and re-read the encouragement of our friends and family on there. I drew strength from their support and communicate with a large amount of people in a short amount of time. I was able to both ask and answer questions simultaneously. It helped sooth and fight exhaustion at the same time.

When I was struggling, I returned to see pictures of him. I watched videos of him when I wanted to hear his voice and see him active and alive again.

It served as a constant reminder that he was real, that he mattered and that I was not the only one who felt this way. That realization, while subtle, was powerful.

I tried to motivate and encourage others, like they'd done for me over the course of the previous year.

This is what that looked like on one particular day:

Was feeling sentimental tonight and wanted to see my boy.

If you find yourself in a funk, chronically feeling sorry for yourself and wondering where God is in your life, I would recommend taking a look at my Facebook profile from January of this year. It is a pretty strong illustration of God's presence on our world and in our individual lives...it took me more than an hour to read two days of posts--amazing and comforting, even through the initial tears.

Don't fret, the tears were quickly suffocated by hope...

One of the many reminders we received on
Facebook. The message that accompanied,
four words: The Moon is Round

Went to a college reunion

Every year, my buddies from college get together two times. The first is the weekend after the fourth of July for a golf tournament in the Kansas City area. The second is the first weekend in December when we camp out on the Meramec River and gig fish. Yes, I said we camp out the first weekend in December. It is tradition, and after 15+ years, it is nearly perfected. Complete with a pig roast, skeet shooting tournament with a consolation bracket and wiffleball game, it is one of the weekends I look forward to every year.

The other weekend I look forward to is the AB Classic-that annual golf tournament. Due to random circumstances, I had missed the previous three years. Every year it goes on the calendar…and every year, something came up at the last minute that cancelled my trip. This year proved to be different and we were finally able to make the trip again.

Every year, on Friday evening, the host couple purchases food for the group and asks everyone who eats to leave whatever money they would've spent on dinner elsewhere to be donated to a designated philanthropy or cause. About 8 weeks prior to the Classic, I got a call from Aaron Bowers (The "B" in AB classic) telling me they would like to give the money they collect from the meal this year to the playground we were building for Grayden at our church. Moved and humbled, I let them know we would be both honored and grateful for the support.

It was a great weekend. I am a terrible golfer, but my team won—and I am counting it. My name will be engraved on the trophy for that particular year. (Of course there is a travelling trophy…if we are going to do something, we are going to do it right.)

That weekend, well over $700 was raised for the playground. I was downstairs when Aaron and his wife gave me the money. He said he didn't want to make a big deal of it, but wanted me to know what had been raised.

I wanted a big deal to be made of it!

This was fantastic. I teared up as I both hugged and thanked him. It was a moment I will never forget. There were a fair amount of tears that weekend as we shared our story numerous times. By this time, the tears were healing for us.

Two days after we returned home, I got a phone call from another of my buddies who we'd stayed with over the weekend. I could hear some excitement in his voice and I thought he was going to tell me that they were having another baby. Instead, he told me that when he returned to work, he told the stories of the weekend to his boss. He went on to say that his boss told him that his company would like to match the money that was raised over the weekend for the playground.

Again, I found myself appreciative, humbled and in disbelief. Almost $1500 was raised to benefit the playground. Once again, our friends (our extended family) were showing their support and refusing to let us do this on our own. Every time we turn around, we are reminded that we are not alone as we move forward—that is a gift directly from God.

Told the devil
to go home

I was not able to sleep until the third night after he died. I felt my body wearing down and knew I needed to sleep.

After a call to my friend, the pharmacist, I figured out an appropriate dose of a sleep aid and at about midnight I thought I might be able to sleep.

In the days leading up to this, I was afraid when I closed my eyes that I would see Grayden when I found him that day…so much so, that I was pretty sure I had set myself up for disaster. The fear of not getting that image out of my head haunted me, and I could not find a way to combat it.

Sure enough, when I laid down and closed my eyes, that was the first thing I saw.

With Jamie asleep beside me, I sat upright in the bed and said aloud, "Go to hell" And then I immediately laughed.

Why?

Well, it was simple: I thought it was hilarious that I told Satan to "go home." I considered my fear and the anxiety I was experiencing about finding him a direct attack from Satan. "Go to Hell" is not a phrase I use…it was not something I had in my back pocket in case I needed it, it was not something I had rehearsed to combat this potential roadblock.

I just reacted…and that was the result.

Funny thing is, I laughed at this, relaxed and slept all night.

Re-told stories about him

I told and re-told stories repeatedly that year. I probably told the same stories to the same people repeatedly as well—but nobody ever stopped me.

Perhaps it was because they didn't have the heart to stop me in my tracks? Maybe it was because they really weren't paying attention so it was not a huge deal? I prefer to believe they liked hearing the stories as much as I liked telling them—that somehow, the stories kept him alive and vibrant in our hearts and minds.

Grayden with his first ever cake

Was overwhelmed
by gifts

This hand-crafted box holds a scrapbook put together by our church community.

People wanted to care for us.

In many instances, they did that by memorializing him. We received numerous physical reminders of his impact on our pasts and his presence in our futures. It's cliché, but while he was gone, he certainly would not be forgotten. It would be impossible to highlight everything people did for us, so I have selected a few: not necessarily our favorites, but ones that will be easy to illustrate.

At the dinner after his funeral, where a meal of macaroni and cheese, peanut butter and jelly sandwiches cut into hexagons, hot dogs, fish sticks and chicken nuggets were served, there was paper on the table for people to share memories of Grayden. Our friends used those to construct a scrapbook. We received the book on the one-year anniversary of his death and it was fantastic.

Our friend Adam made a custom box complete with a crescent moon design to hold the scrapbook. The entire gift was beautiful and will be something we cherish forever.

The "G" puzzle piece charm symbolizes "I love you to pieces."

The puzzle piece necklace was a gift from our friend, Erin. She showed our family an insane amount of love following Grayden's death. It broke her heart on many levels, and I could clearly tell.

She told me about 4 months after the fact, that she wanted me to know that she still thought of him every day. That they still cried with us as they missed him and mourned alongside our family.

She is crafty and creative, and this charm is one of the many gifts she blessed us with over the course of that year. I am grateful for friends like Erin, like many of our friends. The fact that he is remembered means so much to me. I hate that people we care about still hurt from his loss, but there is a strange comfort in knowing we are not alone.

One of Jamie's favorite pictures of Grayden was a snapshot of him on our deck wearing a Superman shirt and bright orange sunglasses. The sunglasses belonged to Katie, a former student turned friend and extended part of our family.

Katie searched for a hexagon stretched canvas and made the painting below that now hangs in our home. With the photo, images of the "Engine Turtles," grilled cheese and the moon, the painting sporting a "G" would've been awesome. With *the* sunglasses he was wearing in the photo adhered to the painting, it was perfect.

Our friend Jen, told us she'd had an idea.

It was an idea that led her to a local jewelry store with a request for a special piece to be constructed. The result was a gold pendant in the shape of the Superman logo that contained a letter "G" in its border. Jen had two specially made, one for Jamie and another for me.

She also told us that they were not solid gold. Instead, they were filled with dried flower petals that came from his grave site. That little piece of information was worth more than gold to us. Whenever I see it, I think of him and am reminded of our little Superman.

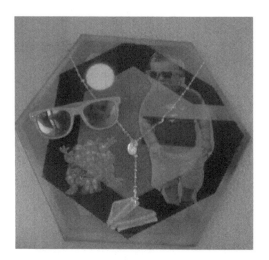

The octagon canvas was a special order. The sunglasses in the picture are the exact ones attached to the original painting from "Aunt Katie" The homemade rosary is a gift from another student and his family.

The Super "G" pendant is the only personalized piece of jewelry I own. It was an original design and is filled with flowers from his grave

Wrote a book and hoped people would want to read it

I heard a lot of people say things like, "You should write a book." And after a while, it started to speak to me.

I knew that I had something to say. And I thought that it might be something that people would be interested in and would want to be able to relate to. I don't know if I was successful in doing that, but that was never really the point.

I put this together because I needed something to focus on. Remembering the last year in this manner was therapeutic for me. I could deal with some things head on and figure out how to best represent them. I was focused and knew the content well. In putting it down on paper, I found that I was able to let go of many of the things that consumed my thoughts.

I hope that this tells the story of a family that struggles, but copes. I hope it provides some semblance of hope in darkness. I hope that it provides understanding to a situation that I pray will never be your reality.

I like attention. But this book is not about attention. It is about healing and common ground. I believe we gain understanding by relating to things that have happened to us directly. While most of our family and friends have not suddenly lost a two year old, they struggled to understand—and that is normal and to be expected. I hope that the stories of a grieving father allow the situation to be more real and more recognizable.

Many have asked me what I could tell them to better handle themselves if they encounter a tragedy in the future. My recommendations are simple, it's ALL in the approach: Ask, Listen and Love.

Ask what they need and offer what you are willing and able to offer—they will let you know what they need and when they need it. Allow them to call the shots and do not be offended if they do not immediately take advantage.

Listen to their stories—they will let you know what is important to them. Relate as you are able and share your comparisons only when asked. Pain can be overwhelming and a silent outlet that is not judgmental is often times greatly appreciated.Love them like you did before—care for them in ways that are natural and sincere. If this is confusing to you, refer to the first two.

These stories are not profound, but they are real. Some of them are beginnings, first steps. Others are memories, bindings for things that will shape me. Their significance will be clearly defined at times, and muddled at others. There is a specific reason each of these stories were shared and I hope you are able to find peace, comfort or suggestion in each.

I am not an expert on grieving. I am however, an expert on *my* grieving. I understand it well…better than anyone as I am the only one who lived it. I cannot write a manual as to how others will respond or handle tragedy. All I can do is share my experience and hope that somehow it is of benefit to you.

Acknowledgements

Thanks to our pastor and friend, Jeremy Irwin, for your many words and guidance that many still continue to be inspired by. You gave us the perfect service for our boy…and we will never forget that.

To our friends from The Journey for your constant love and care

To our grief counselor, Ed Killeen, for leading us through the tough conversations we didn't know how to have on our own

To Melissa Brown…your time and effort made this easier to read

To Ali Bubenik for taking the lead in caring for us…I am so grateful so many followed your lead

Special thanks to Dr. Alan Banaszynski, Dr. Aaron Mohr, Dr. Alehtea Eller, Dr. Cody Tubbs and Dr. Jeanne Sandheinrich for seeing something and treating me

To my buddy, Dave Burgos, for calling everyday…and making sure I was never alone

To Bill Bubenik for book and cover design, formatting this project and making it a reality

To Jamie, Jayce…and now Raelee—for loving your daddy and husband unconditionally…even during the times I was difficult to love.

A note from Grayden's mommy...
Jamie Hickenbottom

As we were mourning the life of another sweet boy gone way too soon, I received a few phone calls asking, "How do we love this family during this time?" Friends, let me help. Here are some things that have kept us going... even years later:

- Don't feel that you have to have something to say. It will come out wrong and it will not help. We know you love us. Hug us. Cry with us.

- Let us tell you the same story over and over again.

- Bring us a warm meal...not just in the few weeks/months after the loss, but in a year, on an anniversary, on a birthday, really any day...we mourn at completely random times.

- Go to Target and walk the aisles with us just to allow us to feel normal for an hour.

- Talk about our child. Even if you think we are having a good day and don't want us to make us cry (we have heard this over and over again), please talk to us about him. Tears are not a bad thing. "If he was worth loving, he is worth grieving over." (Nicholas Wolterstorff, Lament for a Son)

- Tell us your favorite story about our child. Better yet, write down the story and mail it to us. We would love to have it in your handwriting and in your words.

- If you pretend that he never existed, you will hurt us.

- Take my husband to a game, have a game night, smoke a cigar with him, etc and let the conversation turn where it needs to turn. If he needs to break down, encourage it. If he needs to laugh, encourage it.

- Please do not change who YOU are. Be yourself around us.

- Take me for a pedicure and sit in the chair next to me. Bring me a bottle of wine and a romantic comedy and stay to watch it. Cry with me. Listen.

- Do not say anything along the lines of "he's in a better place," "he is never going to have to experience…" I know this, but it does not give us another second with our sweet boy.

- If we choose to have another child, stay close. Our (mostly the pregnant one's) emotions will be all over the place. We will need to talk about difficult things.

- Don't compare your loss to ours to try to relate. Every loss is different.

- Please know that we cannot manage your grief. We want you to mourn with us, but you may need to find another outlet at times.

- Most importantly, continue to pray for us. Our world has been completely rocked. We don't understand, and won't on this side of Heaven. We have moments of anger, hurt, sadness, happiness, etc. We are like freaking rollercoasters of emotions.

I grew up in a Christian home, but Grayden's death has given me a supernatural sense of hope. Heaven has become more real to me because I know Grayden is there. I would never want Grayden to come back to earth after what he has experienced, but instead, I am ready for my family and friends to join him. I am ready to be in a place where "He will wipe away every tear from their eyes, and death shall be no more, neither shall there be mourning, nor crying, nor pain anymore, for the former things have passed away." Revelation 21:4. If you don't know Jesus, please ask us about how he has loved us and has provided for us in more ways than you can imagine.

Many of these ideas come from things that you, our friends, have done for us. Thank you. Thank you for loving our boy. Thank you for loving our whole family. I hope you don't ever have to know this feeling of losing your precious child, but if you do, I will be there. I promise.

Book layout & design by

WEST PARK
CREATIVE

West Park Creative is a comprehensive design boutique offering a specialized range of services. Letterpress Wedding inivtations, print and web design, hand-lettering, logo creation and branding strategies – it's all in our experienced repertoire.

We are a family team working out of St. Louis, Missouri. We occupy the space between your ideas and their creation. We call ourselves artists, creatives, pixel-pushers, wordsmiths, beer-enthusiasts, inkers, nostalgic and everything in between.

westpark-creative.com

23908553R00123

Made in the USA
San Bernardino, CA
04 September 2015